DESTINED *to* BE

Also by Jeff Barnhardt

God of Miracles:
Ordinary People, Extraordinary Stories
www.amazon.com/God-Miracles
-Ordinary-Extraordinary-Stories-ebook/dp/B0786WG4QQ

Destined to Be:
Nine Keys to Live a Life of Purpose
While Unlocking Your Full Potential
www.amazon.com/Destined-Be
-Purpose-Unlocking-Potential-ebook/dp/B01MU6340G

Destined to Be Study Guide
www.amazon.com/Destined-Study-Guide
-Jeff-Barnhardt/dp/1546357572

Destined to Be Facilitator's Guide
www.amazon.com/Destined-Facilitators-Guide
-Jeff-Barnhardt/dp/1546357629

DESTINED *to* BE

NINE KEYS *to* LIVE A LIFE OF PURPOSE
While UNLOCKING YOUR FULL POTENTIAL

JEFF BARNHARDT

Destined to Be

ISBN: 978-0-9958364-0-2
ISBN ebook: 978-0-9958364-1-9

Editor: Jocelyn Drozda
Second editor: Vanessa Carroll
Cover design: Jeff Gifford
Interior design: Beth Shagene

And we know that God causes everything
to work together for the good of those who love God
and are called according to his purpose for them.
ROMANS 8:28 (NLT)

Table of Contents

Acknowledgments

I DEDICATE THIS BOOK TO MY WIFE, ANDREA, WHO HAS SHOWN ME the patience of Job and the love and grace of Jesus. Without her steadfast support, allowing me to spend hours in the pages of this book, I do not believe it would have been possible to write it. For the love she has shown me, the dignity she has afforded me while dealing with my visual impairment, and for the many times she has forgiven me for mistakes I have made throughout our marriage, I thank her.

I would also like to thank my children who have in many ways inspired me to complete this work in hopes it would inspire them to pursue the destiny and calling God has given each of them.

I would also like to thank Jocelyn Drozda for her tireless interpretation of my hilarious dictation software. This no doubt was a long-suffering job for her, and she handled it with professionalism and grace. Well done.

Last but not least, I would like to thank my personal Lord and Savior, Jesus Christ. Without Him, none of this would have ever happened. He found me in the pit and has blessed me with the wife, family, and life I could never have imagined on my own. I give You all the praise and glory!

All the best,
JEFF BARNHARDT

Introduction

As I climbed up on a large rock that day at the hot springs in Ishaka, Uganda, I felt like I was standing at the crossroads of my destiny. Though I came from the ghettos of North America, I was now ministering to the hurting people on the plains of central Africa. This was a surreal experience; one that many in my past would have said was unattainable for me. Countless African tribal people sat in the volcano-heated water they believed could heal them. I knew they were deceived. The only thing that could heal them was a touch from the Lord. As my mind fought against fear, I decided to move forward into what I knew my heavenly Father was calling me to do—preach the gospel to these people who needed it so desperately. The events that happened next were nothing less than miraculous. (I'll tell you the whole story further on in the book.)

That incredible day in Uganda was not a coincidence; it was an opportunity provided by God—a crossroads in my life where I had to make a choice. You reading these words right here, right now is not a coincidence either. It's a confirmation; a confirmation you are in the right place at the right time. In this very moment you are standing at your crossroads; your divine intersection with an opportunity to make a choice. Behind you lay everything you were, and before you lays a promise of everything you could be—your destiny. You were created with a purpose that fuels a desire in your heart, inviting you to be more. Regardless of what anyone has told you, you are not a sum total of all your past experiences and circumstances. You have the opportunity to choose the direction of your life. This book is designed to equip and empower you to be everything that you were created to be. It is my prayer that you will read on and engage with the keys laid out in this book; they will help you discover your purpose and unlock your potential!

Destiny Defined

Throughout the ages, the notion of destiny has intrigued the mind, captured the imagination, and awakened the soul. It is a powerful concept with a depth of meaning as different as each person. We therefore, need to start with the question, "What is your destiny?" When I made this inquiry, a confused look was often the response. Many people have not thoroughly examined this question. On the other hand, when I asked, "What is your dream?" I received responses that culminated in three categories. Putting aside the answers of people with aspirations of being Jedi knights, ninjas, billionaires, or marrying a movie star, the three categories were family, vocation and finances. People believed if they were married, had children, became a professional, or achieved extreme wealth, they would be happy.

The truth is, this is all a mirage. We are bombarded daily with all manners of advertising trying to sell us or tell us what we need to be happy. It is only destiny fulfilled that can truly bring the happiness we so dearly crave. I obtained this truth after many years of tears and pain. I have therefore written this book with the purpose of releasing you from the bondage of your past and present life that may be holding you back from being launched into the pursuit of your destiny. Since the concept of destiny is so unexplored, let's delve a little deeper into it.

The English Oxford Living Dictionary[1] defines destiny as "the events that will necessarily happen to a particular person or thing in the future." It also describes it as "the hidden power believed to control future events." This makes destiny something that is absolutely supposed to happen to you in the future. That being the case, it is crucial to understand what your destiny is and from where it comes. I am fascinated by the paradoxical nature of destiny: seeking something that is to be, but does not exist as of yet. So if destiny is absolutely to happen, yet resides in the future, what are we supposed to do now? How do we know if we are on the right path and if we are making the right decisions? Can destiny be affected by my choices, or is it already so predefined and predetermined that I do not have any role in it at all? These are critically important questions and they will shape who you are and who you will become.

I see destiny as akin to the North Star; a guiding light to push toward, but not a level to achieve or a destination to arrive at in itself. Although you can live from a place of destiny, acquiring both inspiration and strength from it, you are not to live in it. What I mean by this is you cannot just simply live in a dream; you must take conscious steps toward it. I refer to these steps as the process of development, or the journey to your destiny. A process always starts with a plan and entails critical ingredients, including time, resources, and required effort. The journey speaks to the trials, tribulations, and troubles you will undoubtedly encounter along the way.

I have found this to be true in my own life. However, the journey also brings much joy, growth, laughter, and victory. It is an amazing process to experience and one we do not have to walk through alone. If we were shown the fullness of our destiny at the beginning of our journey it may seem unimaginable or even unachievable. This is why we are only given intermittent glimpses of it—little snapshots that reveal parts of a bigger picture. This keeps it within your sights and gives you a vision from which to draw upon. The Bible says, "Where there is no vision, the people perish" (Proverbs 29:18 KJV). We have all had these glimpses; some are just brief flashes or impressions in our mind. Sometimes they have been actual dreams, and still other times they have been relayed to us by people we have met along our path. However, they all connect us back to the same place; this place of an inner longing, or even yearning, to be and do something great.

God created us to be creatures of destiny. He is a big God, with big plans for our lives. We do have free will, and thus can make our own plans, but they will pale in comparison to the things He has for us. This is why when we make a plan and we achieve that specific destination, it is always far less fulfilling than we had imagined and anticipated.

In our dreams at night, we often find ourselves soaring above the housetops, or swimming underwater for miles, unhindered by the lack of oxygen. But upon waking, our daily lives are much more restricted, often by nothing other than our own self-prescribed limitations. We stop the dreams by focusing on our present circumstances that are so different from our dreams. In our present mindsets we allow such things as financial, physical, emotional, or mental limitations to stop us from pushing into the dream. But if we let God reveal His destiny in our lives, it will push us upward to higher heights than we could ever have imagined or attained on our own. This is the essence of destiny. This is what you have been created for!

Destiny versus Destination

Destiny is often confused with destination. A destination is the attainment of a goal along our path or such things as the achievement of a certain desired level of economic or educational status. Destinations are places through which to progress, but not places to remain. Destiny, on the other hand, is a bigger, future call for our lives.

People can be trapped in disillusionment when they arrive at what they believe is their destiny—their plan and purpose for life—yet, in reality, it was only one of the many destination points along their way. It is no wonder that instead of feeling like they had "arrived," the experience became anti-climactic, and they only reaped disappointment.

I experienced this years ago when I became a successful entrepreneur and achieved the status that came with it. Some refer to this as the mountain top experience. I call it destination syndrome. I reached the top of the business mountain and expected to be fulfilled, yet the reality of the achievement seemed much smaller than I thought it would be. What I had thought would happen, did not. It was a mirage. I thought the money, power, and notoriety that came with this achievement would make me happy. It did not. On the contrary, I felt empty and longed for something more.

This can hold true for people in all walks of life, from those in blue-collar and white-collar professions to successful movie and sports stars alike. No one is immune. The sense of disillusionment that people encounter when they arrive at a destination point and find what they thought was going to be there is not, can be devastating. The despair of that encounter explains why we see people achieve a certain level in life, and then begin to deteriorate. It is not a rare occurrence to see the self-inflicted demise of another super-rich, super-famous star splashed across the news media. I believe this happens because they cannot shake the emptiness of arriving at what they thought was their destiny and finding out it was an illusion; there was nothing there. They did not feel fulfilled. Sadly, they had failed to realize their achievement was only a destination, not their destiny. They were built for even greater things that had not yet been actualized.

This is not to say destination points are in any way a negative. They are, in fact, essential checkpoints marking the various stages of your progress as you achieve higher and higher levels along your journey. Achieving these goals or checkpoints can serve as indicators as to whether you are making the right decisions and heading in the right direction to fulfill your greater purpose or whether you need to be realigned. You can choose to make each measure of success a self-serving and self-glorifying purpose, or you can take on a perspective of humility and put your successes back in the hands of the Creator to be used to lift others up and help them along in their journey. This makes the destination point a platform from which to be lifted even higher, onto bigger things—perhaps even into the realm of establishing a legacy to encourage and inspire others, rather than just the simplicity of reaching goals. This being said, it is time to remove the self-imposed limitations and barriers. You are not excluded. You have a wonderful destiny, awaiting fulfillment. No exceptions, not even one!

PART ONE

CHAPTER 1

The Development Process —PART A

Setting the Stage

So what exactly is this amazing destiny that awaits you? Why are you here? Though I don't attest to know the answer to the individual purpose of your life, I do know the One who does. The goal of this book is to provide you with the developmental keys and the right perspective to help you understand the process of connecting with and fulfilling the Creator's plan for your life. To achieve full comprehension of this process, we must start at the beginning, and that is in the book of Genesis.

God created the world. He spoke everything into existence except for one thing, and that was man. God said to Himself, *Let Us create man in Our own image* (see Genesis 1:26). Then God Himself reached down into the dirt with His very own hands and formed man. He breathed the breath of life into him and the man became a living person.

I can only imagine the feeling God had looking at His new son. It causes me to reflect on the birth of my own children. The deep and immediate love I felt for them was overwhelming to the point of tears. I knew instantly I would be willing to do or give anything for them, even my very life. How much more would God the Father feel this deep, inseparable love for His new child? He made the first man, Adam, complete—so complete that everything we would ever need was already in that first man.

As God observed His new son, He saw it was not good that man would be alone. The Bible goes on to say that God caused the man to fall into a deep sleep. While the man slept, God took a rib from his side and created him a woman—his life mate (Genesis 2:21–23). I think it is important to point out that the woman was taken from his side and not from his foot. They were to be co-heirs with a co-destiny. This unity is what the enemy has set himself against. I believe there is an attack on the women in the body of Christ today that is preventing them from engaging in the fullness of their destiny. Men must take a position of empowering women to stand beside them, not behind them. The Bible is clear that the power of two walking in unity is undeniable. Deuteronomy 32:30 describes how one will put one thousand to flight and two will put ten thousand to flight. This exponential increase in power through unity is why the enemy has set himself on dividing men and women since the Garden of Eden.

Originally, God had placed this couple into the garden and told them to have dominion over all the earth and everything in it, and so they did. I can imagine God giving this charge and then saying, "Oh, and one thing ... you see that tree in the middle of the garden ... I don't want you to eat from it, because if you do, you will surely die. Other than that, everything is yours."

I spent many years asking myself why God would put this tree in the middle of the garden if it would cause not only the fall of man, but it would also give entrance to the sin nature and the curse. But one day the answer hit me—free will. If there were no choice given, there would be no free will.

The Lord spoke to me and pointed out the fact that there wasn't just one tree, there were two trees. If you are familiar with the story, you know one was the tree of knowledge of good and evil and the other was the tree of life. It again goes back to choice and free will. In the Bible, God says, "I put before you today life and death, choose life!" (Deuteronomy 30:19 para). God loves us, and will always give us a way out; a better choice. The power of decision is the very essence of free will. Your decisions, whether made in wisdom or not, will guide and even define the outcome of your life. If Adam and Eve had submitted to the Father's will and obeyed His one command to abstain from eating from the tree of the knowledge of good and evil and instead had eaten from the tree of life, which was right next to it, they would have been able to live in eternal bliss and glory in permanent relationship with the Father in the garden.

Unfortunately, the serpent tempted the woman and convinced her to eat the fruit from the tree of knowledge of good and evil. We must be aware that the devil is always trying to speak lies to us as he was to Eve in the garden. Her trouble began when she listened to him and only became worse as she responded and began to rationalize with the serpent. The big take-away here is, *do not listen to the lies of the devil.* Even more importantly, do not speak to him unless you are casting him out of your life. Through the conversation, she rationalized her current situation, and fell prey to the lies. I believe this happened because Eve was looking at it from a natural sense, and in that sense, they would not physically die from eating the fruit. God, however, is an eternal, spiritual being, and His reference to their death was that of their spirit.

Clearly, Adam was not innocent either. He stood complacently by and allowed her to converse with the devil and eat the fruit. Then seeing she did not die, he ate of it himself. Sadly, they chose death. With this choice, Adam surrendered all of his authority and dominion over the earth to the devil. Adam and Eve chose rebellion rather than submitting to God's will and obeying His command not to eat from the tree. This caused the fall of man and allowed the sin nature to enter in. This leads us to the first key of discovering your purpose and unlocking your potential: submission and obedience.

DEVELOPMENTAL KEY 1: Submission and Obedience

The concept of submission and obedience is revolutionary and even countercultural in our "me first" society. It is an intentional plan of the enemy to drive us to focus on ourselves, to stop us from engaging with our destiny.

If Adam and Eve had submitted their will to the Father's will, they would not have disobeyed. The sin nature and the subsequent curse would not have entered the world. However, the sin of rebellion ushered in shame and consequently allowed the curse to enter the earth. This curse then spanned the generations and spawned fear. Fear causes anxiety and anger, among many other things, all of which inhibit us from walking in our destiny.

If you stop and reflect, you can see how it is played out in our lives. When we make a bad decision and choose sin, shame settles in as soon as we have committed the act. But shame doesn't come alone. It brings its bedfellow, condemnation, and tries to drive us away from God. The further away from God we become, the easier it is to slip deeper into sin. This perpetual cycle of sin, shame, and condemnation makes us feel like we are trapped in this fallen state, forever destined to repeat it over and over again. But that is not what God has for us. The fall of Adam and Eve was not a surprise to God. It is clear in Ephesians 1:4–5 that it was God's plan before the creation of the world to adopt us into his family through His Son, Jesus.

So God sent His only begotten Son to redeem His creation and restore our ability to have choice. When Jesus died on the cross and shed His blood for us, He provided a way for sin to be forgiven and shame to be removed. It is through the blood of Jesus that God extended to humanity His forgiveness and grace. His forgiveness frees us from the bondage of sin and the weight of shame. His grace empowers us to overcome the sin nature we were born with and walk in the freedom that was paid for at the cross. If we commit our lives to Christ and submit to His plan, this act of obedience will allow us to be propelled by forgiveness and grace, rather than fear. This opens the door to the Father's blessing: His peace, and self-control in our lives—the opposite of the destiny inhibiting anxiety and anger that fear promotes. Although forgiveness and grace are instant, it takes time to work out the shame and condemnation that came from our disobedience, as well as the hurt, pain, and all the other things brought in with it.

You may never have committed your life to Christ and submitted your will to His. Or perhaps you have in the past, but you need to recommit your life. Let's take a minute and pray so you can surrender your heart to the Father. By reading this prayer, I believe a miracle will happen in your life and you will spend eternity with God.

"Dear Jesus, I believe You died on the cross for my sin, and through your death You have extended to me forgiveness and grace. Please forgive me of my sin and come into my heart. Be the Lord of my life. In Jesus' name, I pray. Amen." If you prayed that prayer for the first time or recommitted your life, the Bible says old things are passed away and all things are made new (2 Corinthians 5:17 NKJV). You are born again! Right now is a new beginning for you. Remember, the shame, condemnation and all the things from your past will still take time to sort out. This in itself is a journey. Enter the necessity of the development process.

This process reminds me of making shoebox cameras in grade seven shop class. To make the cameras, we took an old shoebox and cut a small, square hole of approximately a quarter inch by a quarter inch, in one end. We then fashioned a three-inch-long by one-inch-high piece of cardboard that slid back and forth in front of the hole, to create an aperture. We then placed a piece of film inside the box to capture our picture, put the lid on the box, and took it out to a field. We took several different types of pictures by sliding the small piece of cardboard to open the hole and allow the light to flood in and capture the image it saw. Once the task was completed, we took the shoebox into the shop's darkroom to develop the piece of film, now called a negative.

In the darkroom there were several chemical solutions, and we placed the negative in each solution for a certain amount of time to develop them. If we left the negative in too long, it would become over exposed. If we took it out too soon, it would be underdeveloped. If we had perfect timing, we were able to develop the image to accurately reflect the original picture taken outside.

Perhaps you are saying right now, "What does this have to do with the fall and redemption of man?" Well, let's look at the definition of "image." Remember, God said He was going to make man in His own image. The Merriam-Webster online dictionary[2] defines the word image as an optical counterpart of an object produced by an optical device, such as a lens or mirror, or an electrical device. What this means is that in the beginning, when creating us, He was actually making us into the image of Himself through Jesus. Adam was never the original plan.

In the Beginning

The best way I've heard this development process described is by Bishop T.D. Jakes at the Man Power Conference. He explains that in the beginning there was the Father, the Son, and the Holy Spirit. We can think of the Father as the Photographer, standing at the beginning of time looking through His viewfinder at the end of time, where He sees the perfect and complete image of man, His Son, Jesus Christ. In Christ, He sees you fully developed and perfect in every way. Jesus, who is the Alpha and the Omega, the beginning and the end, the perfect image of man, was the plan from the beginning of time. Adam was never the final plan. It was Jesus and His shed blood on the cross for our sins that would bring us into right relationship with the Father, allowing Him to see us as perfect in every way, right from the beginning.

Since in Christ, the Father sees us in our final, perfect image, He clicks the button by simply speaking the word, causing it to explode into existence. He sends out the light, the Holy Spirit, to capture the image. He superimposes the DNA of the final image on the film and you are born.

Just like in traditional photography, the final image of you is superimposed on the film to create the negative. The negative is the reversed image of the end picture. We come into the world in this format because of the aforementioned fall of man and the consequential sin nature. It is the exact opposite of the final picture while retaining in it all the characteristics required to produce that final glorious image. It only needs to be put through the development process to extract the final image that the photographer saw at the point of capture.

To do this, God, the Master Developer, allows this negative to go into a darkroom to begin the process of development. This is not to say God becomes a force of destruction in our lives. On the contrary, we have an enemy of our destiny who is responsible for every evil thing. Our enemy does not want us to go through this process, and we will discuss that and the darkroom process in much greater detail in other chapters. However, God is sovereign, and He does allow us to go through these processes so we can become everything He intended us to be. He will cause all these things to work together for our good in this development process. God knew the first man was going to fall, and as a result, as previously stated, He had the recovery plan for the redemption of our lives from the very beginning: the development of a negative through His son, Jesus.

This may be difficult to understand, but do not worry, for God is a Master Photographer and a Master Developer. What He saw in you from His perspective was everything you would become in the fulfillment of your destiny in the fullness of Christ. When you look at the negative, it is much smaller than the original picture. This makes your destiny much, much bigger than your humble beginnings. It is through the process of development—those situations when you feel like you are going through hell—that you will be enlarged. Your vision and your destiny will be expanded to the full extent of the original curator's perspective.

I find it fascinating that to create a film negative, the image is superimposed onto a transparent piece of plastic as to not affect the image in any way. This means that everything the final picture requires, or the fulfillment of your destiny, is already encased in who you are when you are born. The process of development is simply drawing out the characteristics, giftings, attributes, and abilities already placed in you from the beginning of time by the Creator of everything. There are no additional ingredients required. The creation, in exactly the way you have been made, is fully complete. You can do nothing to make the picture any better than it already is. Your only requirement is to say "yes" and to yield yourself to the process, and to the Master Developer.

In our modern era, digital photography has become the mainstay when it comes to taking pictures. Click the button and poof! The images are fully developed, and that's it. In our microwave society, we don't want to wait for anything. We don't want to allow patience to have its perfect work. We don't want to go through any darkrooms or have to go through a painstaking development process. This culture of instant gratification is very apparent in society today in so many areas.

The weight loss industry is an excellent example of this. It is constantly trying to sell you the latest gadget guaranteed to help you lose all the weight you want, simply by using it for five minutes a day while watching TV and eating chocolate—in three weeks none the less, or your money back! Couple that with the prepackaged meals, shakes, and other fad diets, and you can see how it has become a multi-billion-dollar industry in North America today. People are drawn to these methods of weight loss because it's quick and easy. They are not required to do anything, let alone eat right and exercise. We want it done, and we want it done now, with as little pain, struggle, or effort as possible. But this is not how God works, although He could if this was what He wanted. Not even in the creation of the universe did He just wave His hand and make it all appear. Instead, He chose to take His time and delight in the creation process. He did this even more so with man, making it an intimate and intentional act of love. Our Father is an eternal being. As a Master Developer, He will take His time, the perfect time, to pull out the fullness of that original image.

Although this part of our walk doesn't sound like the epitome of enjoyment, the truth is, the glory of the final image is so wonderful that every single step of the process of development is not only used for our benefit, but is worth it in the end. It is through this process that the Lord pulls out and refines the characteristics of the final image. In other words, He can teach us things, from a character development perspective, through our hard times that we perhaps may be unable to learn in any other manner. I am not saying that God causes bad things to happen to us. On the contrary, He will cause all things to work together for good. As a marathon runner, I can attest to the fact that the hours of painstaking training, sore muscles, and the like are worth it the second you cross the finish line and receive your finisher's medal! How much greater will it be to cross the finish line at the end of our life's race and receive the crown of life?

God has a deep love for His creation, and He has a master plan for our development. His plan will take you through all the processes needed, and growth will become a significant part of your life. This is the journey to your destiny!

CHAPTER 2

The Development Process —PART B

The Darkroom

The journey to your destiny starts with the Father, the Son, and the Holy Spirit working together in the development process of the negative, which is you, to bring about the fulfillment of the complete picture, which is you walking in your destiny. I have suggested this process is very similar to how natural film is developed and that it begins in the darkroom.

The darkroom represents the trials and tribulations we encounter throughout our lives. There are many different types of trials we go through, challenges we must face, and hurts we must overcome. Some are bearable, while others almost push us to the brink of insanity. Some people experience darkrooms of physical, emotional, or sexual abuse. Sometimes it is a serious injury or illness. It could also be the loss of a loved one. I have had countless darkroom experiences in my life, and many of them I had to face as a child.

Much of what happened to me while growing up I considered evil. At times, I even wondered how God could allow me to go through such things. I recognize that God does not cause these things, but He definitely allows them. He is a sovereign God who can do anything, including preventing us from going through any situation. But remembering that God is a Great Developer and a Master Strategist, He will not let any situation go to waste.

In Romans 8:28, it is clear that God causes all things to work together for good, whether we understand it or not. Or, it could be said He causes all things to work together in our development process. It also says He causes what the enemy intended for evil, to be used for good. Now I have come to recognize that many of my life experiences have been an extensive process of development.

As we journey through this book together, I will lay bare my soul and share some of my greatest tragedies and mightiest triumphs in the exploration of this process. One of these accounts, the one I share now, I can say without the risk of over exaggeration, was a more than traumatic darkroom.

From the Darkroom into the Light

I come from extremely humble beginnings. I had a very difficult childhood in a dysfunctional family where abuse was the norm. I was the second youngest of seven children. Through all of these difficulties, there was one person, my big brother Doug, who was always there for me. Doug was a kind, big-hearted guy who was ten years older than I was. Throughout the years of growing up, it was Doug who looked out for me. He would often step in and protect me in times of abuse. I remember as a little boy—I was maybe three or four years old—how I would cuddle up underneath his blankets so I would feel safe from the surrounding chaos that was my home life. He used to call me his little teddy bear.

One time while I was in grade three, I was being bullied. A grade six boy picked me up and dropped me headfirst into a trash can. He did this in the midst of a playground full of kids, who were jeering and laughing at me. It took some time to struggle out of that garbage can, and when I did, I ran home crying. Doug saw me in this state as I entered the house, and asked me what happened. Through my tears, I told him. He grabbed me by the hand, and we marched straight back to the school and found the kid who did this to me. Being in the militia, Doug was a tough looking, big guy, so when he had a good talk with the bully, needless to say, nothing ever happened again. Actually, I had a great rest of the year with a newfound respect in that school.

When Doug eventually moved out of the house to start his own life and family, I felt a great sense of loss. Something was definitely missing in my life. There was now a big hole where my brother had been. After Doug had left, I was on my own. This is when some of my first memories surfaced of being so alone. I remember hiding underneath my bed crying. My dad was yelling and breaking things, so there I hid, hoping he wouldn't find me. With my brother gone, all I had to hold on to was a little teddy bear. That bear became very special to me.

Not many years later, when I was sixteen years old, our family suffered a house fire in which my room was completely gutted. I lost everything I had owned up to that point. I remember going into the charred house, and I could only think that this must be what hell looked like: melted pictures, scorched walls, and smoke escaping through holes that the firefighters had chopped.

I walked into my room, and my heart sank. There he was—my special little bear—my panda bear that had been given to me for Christmas when I was five years old, now destroyed by the fire. I had asked for this bear for many months before Christmas, and when I received him on Christmas morning, I was ecstatic. I remember running around the house hugging and playing with this very special bear. I also remember many nights full of yelling and tears, when I would hold on tight to that same bear, while snuggling up with my brother Doug. And then when he left, it was just me and my bear. This little panda bear was one of my last comforts. He was now gone, and so was that chapter of my life.

I was sixteen at this point, and I decided to leave and strike out on my own. Of course, I quickly found my brother, and for a couple of years we were inseparable; doing life together once again. I had experienced many of my firsts in life with him, and we had a lot of fun doing such things, like traveling across the country. Doug and I had a tight relationship, but when I was eighteen years old, we hit a rough patch. We had never fought before, but there was a situation with a girl he knew, and it caused our first argument.

I was becoming a young man who was developing his own opinions, and I disagreed with what he was doing. I told him so. On the way out of my apartment that day, he looked me straight in the eyes, and the only way I can describe it is that I saw darkness. His eyes were sinking back into his head, and I could tell he was in trouble. I suggested he get out of town for a while and let things cool down. That is when he slapped me across the face, said a couple of words, and walked away. I didn't see him for the next two weeks. This was devastating to me because up to that point, we did almost everything together.

Then the night of December 13, 1996 came. This night is forever etched in my brain. I can clearly hear the phone ring in my mind just as it happened that day. My other brother Robert was on the other end of the line, and I could tell by the tone in his voice that something was horribly wrong. All he said was, "Jeff, have you heard?"

I replied, "Heard what?"

"Doug is dead."

I literally dropped the phone to the floor and screamed out in anguish, "NOOOOO!" I had heard mothers on TV scream out like this when their babies had died. Before this, I didn't understand their reaction. Regretfully, now I understood it.

Doug and I had been in many difficult situations together through the years and now that I was older I had been able to watch his back as much as he had watched mine in the past. So the fact I was not there when he was stabbed and he subsequently died alone, was extremely difficult for me. He was murdered in the throes of gang violence. He left behind a beautiful wife and two sweet daughters. That night my heart was heavy with guilt. My mind began to race. I asked myself, *Why did I fight with him? Why wasn't I there with him? If I had been there, he wouldn't be dead today.* I knew the guy who killed him, and this compounded my pain.

This event sent me into a downward spiral of addictions, and I ended up homeless on and off for the next four years. During the latter part of these years, I tried to straighten out my life, but I came from a non-Christian family and did not know God, so I was on my own. All I had to turn to were my addictions.

In 1999, I ended up working at a discount store selling computers. The first few months were great. I had a place to live, and I went to work each day dressed in my Value Village shirt and tie. I was a good salesman, so I was making decent money. But my addiction soon caught up to me, and I found myself as a functional addict. This meant that I would work during the day, but I would yield to my addiction at night. I quickly found myself back on the street with nowhere to go.

One night when I was out on the street without a place to sleep, I began to think about my life. That is when I heard for the first time, what I know now as the voice of the Holy Spirit. He told me to call John. I quickly played out that scenario in my mind and knew I could not do it. John worked at the same store I did, and if I called him and said I had nowhere to go, my façade would be blown. But as it grew darker and colder, I relented to the persistent voice that bid me give him a call. On a payphone, I made the call. As he answered, I said, "John, this is Jeff," and with a crackling in my voice I continued, "I have nowhere to sleep tonight."

All he said was, "Where are you?" I told him, and he said, "Do not move. I'll be there in twenty minutes." It turned out John was a Christian, and he lived in the basement suite of a pastor's house. They began to tell me about Christ and what He did for me on the cross. I had never heard this before, and my acceptance of this truth was my first step, or should I say, first choice in my development process and the beginning of my journey.

Joseph's Darkroom

The Bible gives us many clear examples of this concept of development in the darkroom as well. Looking at the life of Joseph (Genesis 37–41), it is clear that he went through many darkrooms in his lifetime. As he shared with his brothers the glimpses he was given of his incredible destiny, they became murderously jealous. They would not accept their place in it, so they did everything they could to thwart it, first throwing him into a pit (his first recorded darkroom experience), and then selling him into slavery. Even his father, who loved him dearly, was angry at him for believing in his own destiny.

On a side note, as people misunderstood Joseph, people too, may misunderstand you and your pursuit to fulfill your destiny. You must not let this dissuade you from the pursuit of what you are called to do. Be sure to share your destiny dream with only those who will speak life into it. Matthew 7:6 (NKJV) reminds us not to cast our pearls before swine. It is imperative to push through to what God has created you for. You have no idea who you may impact and how you will change the world, just as Joseph literally changed the world during his time.

Joseph started extremely far from his destiny as he sat in the pit he was thrown into, a very literal darkroom, where he waited, probably scared and anxiously wondering if his father would come to rescue him. It would also be reasonable to assume he questioned how God could give him such a grandiose vision, and yet he found himself here in this cold, dark pit. At the time, he would not have known he was being developed for something great. His brothers did come to remove him from his pit, but rather than restoring him and asking for forgiveness, they sold him into slavery, and freedom eluded him once again. I can only imagine the destitute feelings that tried to overtake him as he faced losing everything that was dear to him.

As Joseph found himself in the house of Potiphar (Genesis 39), he was indeed in another darkroom. Though the Bible does not say how Joseph responded, I think it is very clear he did not throw himself a pity party. He didn't call all his associates and relatives and tell them of his sufferings. Instead, he pressed in and began to build a new life for himself, which seemed to have great promise.

This is an important truth to understand. Your response to the darkroom will determine many things about your experience in it. You can lengthen it, artificially shorten it, and even diminish its effectiveness. I believe the most beneficial way to deal with the darkroom experience is to yield to the Master Developer.

Paul provides the key to this when he says to be content in all things (Philippians 4:12). This allows patience to produce its perfect work and for you to become fully developed. I am not saying this is easy or even enjoyable. On the contrary, it may be one of the most difficult things you've ever had to do in your life. But the Word promises He is causing all things to work together for your good. Allowing His Word to be a lamp unto your feet in the darkroom and stepping through it with God one step at a time, will lead to your full development.

As the Lord was with Joseph, he rose from the lowly position of slave to being in charge of everything Potiphar owned. Then, in an instant, just as Potiphar's wife snatched his coat off his back, his entire life was snatched away from him again, and he was cast into the next darkroom: a prison—sent there because of unjust accusations and his choice of honor and faithfulness over adultery and sin.

I am sure Joseph was thinking, *What's going on here, God?* I'm sure he was crying out, attesting to his faithfulness and innocence. I am sure he began to question whether or not the visions he was given were actually an insight into his destiny, or simply a weird dream from eating too much cheese or something! We might think Joseph would begin to question whether God was even real at this point.

No, not Joseph. Instead, he remained patient and faithful. He began to rebuild his life once again, pushing on toward his destiny, this time being put in charge of everything that happened in the prison. This provided an interesting opportunity for Joseph when the king's cup bearer and the baker were put under his charge in the prison. Rather than complaining about how difficult his life had been, recounting the many infractions committed against him and the injustices he had suffered, he sat and listened to their dreams. He served and ministered to them presumably in moments that were significant darkrooms in their lives and interpreted their dreams for them. Unknowingly, in doing so he found the key to unlocking the final steps and his destiny.

Like Joseph, we all will be presented many opportunities and choices to make throughout our journey of development. We can choose to go through our process with negativity and complaining, or we can choose to keep a positive attitude and take the steps put before us. Often these steps teach us important lessons in our journey. If we choose not to take this path and learn the lessons, we will continue to go around and around and around until we pass that test.

The Bible clearly illustrates this as we see the Israelites wandering in the desert for forty years to complete a journey that should have taken three days. All of this unproductive time resulted from their decision not to do the task that was set before them and enter the Promised Land as the Lord commanded. Instead, they let fear grip their hearts and unbelief overtake them. They complained about their situation rather than pressing in. There is a powerful lesson to be learned here. The fruits of your effort may not always be instantaneous, but they will be there.

Joseph did not make the same mistake as the Israelites. His story thus became much different than theirs. He was able to interpret the dreams of the cup bearer and the baker for them, but was forgotten in return. (When you are removed from your darkroom into your destiny, don't forget about your friends and family, the ones who walked with you along the way. Joseph did not forget about his family in the end.) I can imagine the conversation he had with God when he was forgotten: "Lord, what are You doing to me? Why are you keeping me in this prison? I have served You. I have done everything You have asked, and I'm still in chains! What did I do to deserve this? You showed me this destiny filled with greatness. You said I would be a great leader of nations, and now look at me! I'm just a pitiful prisoner!"

Though the Bible does not clearly tell us what the conversation actually was between Joseph and God, it does tell us he remained faithful. In the same way, your response to your darkroom will dictate how high God can elevate you in the process. Sometimes you have to go under in order to go over. Sometimes you have to submit your dream and serve someone else in the season you are in for a time, in order to see your own destiny fulfilled. You may have to go low to go high. While Joseph was in this season, he rolled up his sleeves and began to serve in whatever capacity he could.

And then an amazing thing happened. In an instant, he went from the jail cell to the palace. Just think, one day you're a prisoner, and the next you're the prime minister. Now that is fruit! Not only will God take you and place you in front of the king, He will also give you everything you need in order to be able to do what you need to do in that situation.

Only God, the Master Developer, could have seen the picture He was developing through the entire life of Joseph. What would have happened if Joseph were to have given up at any point throughout his development process? Not only would his life have been lost, but the entire nation of Israel would have been lost as well. This includes Jesus Himself. Of course, God could have raised up the nation of Israel again, but Joseph, through the fulfillment of his destiny, saved the nation and the people of Israel. Wow!

The testament in the story of Joseph is that in all the darkrooms, in all the difficulties Joseph endured, and in all the solutions he used to resolve the desperate situations he faced, it was all training for him to fulfill his final destiny as the prime minister of Egypt. It is often said God will use your mess and turn it into a message. This is the underlying theme of the story of Joseph, and it is what makes his story so truly inspirational.

His Solution

As we come into a full understanding of how God uses the darkroom in the process of our development, it is important to realize this is only one part of the process. The second part of the process involves

God's timing. We can liken that to the duration of development necessary to produce the perfect photograph.

To bring out different attributes of the photo, the negative is placed in a chemical solution. This solution would correlate to the situations that are happening to you while you are going through your trials on your journey. Like I recounted earlier, if the developer removes the negative from the solution too soon or leaves it in too long, it'll either become under exposed or over developed. Each of these outcomes will ruin the negative and thus destroy the end picture.

How many times have we asked God to intervene in a situation when we believed we could withstand it no longer? But we have to remember, God is the Master Photographer and Developer and His timing is perfect. He will not leave you in any situation for too long, nor will He rescue you prematurely. He will keep you there as long as it is required for you to be carefully developed. We see this in the life of Jesus the night before his crucifixion. His prayer in the garden to the Father was, "If it be your will, let this cup pass from me" (Matthew 26:39). I can imagine the Father himself looking down at His Son saying, "If I were to remove you now, you would not become fully developed and fulfill your destiny as the Savior of the world." As Christians, are we not eternally grateful that God the Father did not remove Jesus from the darkroom of His crucifixion before the appointed time?

This is why patience and endurance for the process are so crucial. The Bible says in James 1:4, "But let patience have its perfect work, that you may be perfect and complete, lacking nothing" (NKJV). You can have faith and trust that God will remove you from every hardship at the perfect time, and that He will not allow you to endure something that would be crushing to your destiny.

It can be difficult for us as humans to come to terms with how a loving God can allow us to endure the things that hurt us and cause us pain. As a father of four, I have come to understand that in order for my children to be developed so they can fulfill their own destinies, some of the situations or scenarios they may have to go through will be painful for them, and equally, if not more so, painful for me as a father to watch.

All of us, including our children, must endure various situations to build character and be developed. There are many times when I want to swoop in and rescue them. Sometimes that may be appropriate, but in other situations, it would be to their detriment. How much more so would our Heavenly Father want to intervene, but He does not want to remove us prematurely from the darkrooms and the solutions that will develop us, so the Holy Spirit can have His perfect work.

On the other side of that situation is remaining in the solution too long. God may be speaking to us, asking us to share Jesus with our neighbor or co-worker. Or maybe He is saying get involved in a project of our local church. Perhaps He wants us to go to Africa, or even treat our spouse in a different way. I don't know specifically what God is speaking to you about, but I know the Holy Spirit speaks, and sometimes He is asking us to do something … and we don't move! There are times you have to go. You have to step out and take the risk. Trust that you are ready when He says you are ready, and move!

CHAPTER 3

The Enemy of Your Destiny

As much as God the Father and His team want your destiny in Christ Jesus to be fulfilled, the enemy, the devil, does not. Simply put, this is because you will then have the power to crush him beneath your feet. The ground you take when you become all God has designed for you to become, is ground that he has to give up to you and to the Kingdom of God. He will even go so far as to concede some ground if it means you will stop pushing forward in your destiny. It is the same strategy used in modern day firefighting. The firefighters will burn certain sections of trees to make a fire break. This will stop the advancement of the flames, and prevent them from consuming any more territory, which keeps the losses to a minimum.

We see how the enemy uses this tactic in Luke 4. When Jesus was in the wilderness for forty days, the devil revealed to Him all the kingdoms of the world. He tried to tempt Jesus into walking away from His calling as Savior of the world by offering Him the glory of these kingdoms. Although the devil would have had to give up these kingdoms and any authority he had over them, he would have won a far bigger battle in the end.

This is exactly what he will try to do with you. He will try to set up an exchange with things and people, such as a spouse, children, or even a desired career, to contain you. All of these things in themselves are good, but if they stop you from pushing forward in your destiny, they are not prioritized properly in your life. This was evident in my life at one time.

My wife and I started our business in 2007 with a $10,000 loan. We operated it all from our house. I had a driver who drove me to each of my sales appointments. I sold security systems all day and into the evening. Returning home and waking my wife, she would process the paperwork before returning to bed. In the mornings, the delivery driver would transport the equipment to our garage and our two technicians would pick up the equipment and install the security systems. This was truly a business that was started out of a garage.

The driving force in my life at this point was to make sure the business was successful. I did this, but I did it at a great cost to both my family and to the plan God had for my life. It really hit me hard one day while I was watching home movies with my family. In every single video, no matter what the kids were doing, amongst their silliness and giggling, you could hear me in the background on the phone talking business. I was oblivious to what was going on around me. My children were growing up and I was too busy to see or to care.

I would leave and be gone for most of the day working, and when I came home I'd be doing business again, stealing time away from my family and from God. A deep conviction began to fall on my heart as I sat on the couch with them that day, realizing how much of their lives I had missed. At that point, I began to reevaluate my life—what I wanted to do and where I wanted to go. It became clear to me I was spending my whole life on the business, and although it gave me temporary happiness when success came, my business did not love me back. My wife and I would often fight because of it, and the kids were paying the price of an absentee father who was living right in the house with them.

I decided to change my priorities and put God first, my wife second, and then my family third. My business now would come after all of that. This was a significant shift for me, but that decision began to bear fruit after a few months, as our family life began to slowly improve. We are not perfect, but we are much happier today than we were back in those days. We refer to them as "those dark days."

The adventure God has us on today, as a family, is much better than what we had back then. The business is still successful, but it is unquestionably not the priority anymore. In your life too, God and your destiny, or dare I call it, your "obedience to God's plan for your life," should be number one. All of these other things, although important, should be secondary. It is important to understand that by you fulfilling your destiny, you will be exceedingly beneficial to everything and everyone around you. This is simply because you will be doing everything in your life connected to the power you get from your destiny—the power of God. You are allowing God to add His super to your natural. This will make you a better spouse, a better parent, a better business owner . . . the list goes on.

That being said, you are also not called to sacrifice everything else in your life on the altar of destiny. This is not what God intends either. It's about priorities and balance. You must have them set straight so you can serve in all the different parts of your life, along with your vision. It is not acceptable, nor is it God's plan for you to use "pursuing my destiny" as an excuse to be an absentee spouse or parent or to neglect any other important areas of your life. This false belief can become addictive and highly dangerous. However, as you yield to God and His plan for your life, He will give you the strength and grace to be able to wisely prioritize and balance all the important aspects of your life.

Jeremiah 29:11 promises you that God has a plan for you and your life and that is to bless and prosper you. The Scriptures also say if you ask your earthly father for bread, he would not give you a stone, so how much more so does our heavenly Father know how to give good gifts to His children (Luke 11:11–13). The enemy, however, wants you to accept something far less than the best God has for you.

Referring back to the process of film development analogy, if you leave the negative in the solution for too long, it becomes overexposed, thus ruining the final picture. This potential trade off the enemy proposes is a way to keep you in the development process too long. This is often duplicated in the natural realm and is similar to what I often say to my children when they want to have too much candy or ice cream or watch too much of one particular television show. Although what they are doing or what they want may be good, too much of a good thing is a bad thing.

We see this situation appear in endless ways in the world around us. For example, if you were to eat too much ice cream you would become obese. Being obese would restrict you from being able to work, to play with your children, and to perform many other daily activities, thus becoming a bad thing. I see this same principle being re-enacted time and time again in the business field.

In my sales jobs, I would often find myself across the kitchen table from a customer who had been living in the same house for sometimes forty to fifty years or more. Part of my qualification process was to learn about them and to do this I had to ask questions. This brought up many interesting points about peoples' lives. The better I became at my job and the less I had to focus on the presentation I was giving, the more interested I became in their lives. What I learned was that many people are pushing through every single day in the hopes of achieving the life-long dream of retirement. Many people would stay at a job they hated for years, or even decades, so they could qualify for their pension and thus retire. Often, for them retirement meant being able to sit and watch TV instead of working. Or, if they were very fortunate, they could go somewhere warm for a couple of months of the year.

I'm not saying that loyalty to a job or living in one house for a long time is a bad thing. Actually, it is a good thing to be loyal and to have good roots where you live. But remember, too much of a good thing is a bad thing. This was the entirety of their lives.

I often wondered what these peoples' lives would have been like if they had decided to follow their dreams, grasping onto something that ignited passion in their lives. If they were believers, what would have happened if they had connected with God's plan for their life? But regretfully, that is not how it went for them. This caused me to decide to live my life in a different way; to pursue bigger visions, dreams, and goals. In other words, to pursue God's incredible plan for my life.

I believe the enemy is looking to stifle us in the same way in the spiritual realm. Too much of a good thing is a bad thing. If the enemy can get you camping in this unbalanced position, you can become overexposed, and the final picture will not be realized. Unfulfilled destinies and failing to expand the Kingdom of God will be the unintentional consequences. Staying in one step of the development process longer than intended is not part of God's plan. It is not living in the fullness of Christ as He has promised you.

Chasing the Wrong Rabbit

Just as staying in the developing solution too long can be harmful, exiting too quickly can be just as destructive. This distraction strategy of the enemy attempts to overwhelm you with multiple opportunities. In the book *Good to Great,* Jim Collins writes that companies do not die from lack of opportunity; rather they drown in the multitude of them.[3] This concept is just as true for people as it is for a business. I believe this is a tactic of the enemy to stop you from focusing on what you are called to do in your life. This fits with the old, Russian proverb that warns if you chase too many rabbits you will not catch any of them. This has been proven true in my life. It is not hard for any of us to get caught up in this distraction. I did, and I paid the price.

I have always been a bit of a technology geek. I love new software and the latest gadgets. As a visionary, I am always thinking about what could be. Twelve months after we opened our business, it was clear that there was no appropriate software available to do what we wanted to have done. So, I hired a developer and began to develop proprietary software in-house. It was low risk, and it worked. We developed a pretty nice piece of software that served us well.

Five years later, my family, my company and other things in my life were running smoothly. My feet began to itch, and I began to get bored. Looking back, I know now what I viewed as boredom was actually a season of my development process in which I was being built up from the inside. This type of season can be particularly difficult and somewhat deceiving. There can thus be a temptation to get distracted because there is a lack of concrete evidence of God's plan unfolding in your life. The truth is He is still developing you; you just don't realize it. He is actually strengthening you so you will be able to handle the next step in your growth.

Now back to my boredom. A new opportunity presented itself to me. I knew that I could create more efficiency with my business if I build out the proprietary software system we had developed in-house. With more developers it could be produced faster, and I could even sell it to all the other companies in my industry. Wow! What an opportunity! This would mean I would have to strike up a new business and hire staff.

This new company would be a software business, and that was much more exciting than what I was presently doing. So without seeking counsel, I ventured out and opened this company. I did not pay any heed to Proverbs 11:14 that tells us there is safety in a multitude of counselors. Without boring you with details and preventing myself from reliving the pain, two and a half years and a half million dollars later, the ill-fated company was wound down and closed. After reflecting on this for some time, I realized this venture divided me so I could no longer give one hundred percent to anything. As a result, not only did this company fail, but my main business, my bread-and-butter, was also suffering. I had to turn my attention back to my company and begin to rebuild. When I started down that road, it had seemed very attractive to me. But it ended up being a costly distraction, and one I could have done without.

You may have experienced this in your own life in different ways. Perhaps a new job posting presents itself—one that seems so ripe with opportunity, one in which you would be so much more appreciated by your colleagues and management. I have witnessed this in my business. We would often receive an abundance of résumés when we posted a job opening. The applicants who held only short-terms jobs were automatically passed over. We were looking for somebody who could show commitment, a person in whom we could invest, not a job hopper.

This is what I see when it comes to the process of development: many people want to hop from solution to solution, looking for the quick fix or the perfect situation. This may include the ill-advised strategy of jumping from one church to another or going from conference to conference. There is no quick way to complete the development process. It is a process you will endure for the entirety of your life for the benefit of God and His Kingdom. He delights in preparing His bride and developing you to your fullness in Him.

The same disastrous choice can be made in relationships. Perhaps you are in a turbulent marriage, and suddenly you find yourself attracted to someone else who comes into your life. You see them as a more suitable spouse. You start second-guessing yourself and the choices of your past. You see this new person as an opportunity to set yourself free from the difficult situation you are in. Voices are happy to whisper in your heart and mind how unfair things are to you, and how you deserve so much better. "And besides," you say, "the Lord wants me to be happy . . ."

People can bounce from person to person to person or even from marriage to marriage, leaving behind a wake of destruction that would include broken hearts, broken families, and broken lives. This type of behavior also leaves you, as an individual, underdeveloped, feeling desperate, empty, and alone because you are not fulfilling the plan God has for your life. With this type of behavior, most often you end up in a worse situation than when you began, forcing you to start the cycle once again. However, please note I am not advocating that somebody remain in an abusive situation by any means. This is why seeking God in all things is so vital.

I do strongly believe that God does present us with new jobs, new relationships, and new opportunities in which to grow and develop. They very well may be a part of your journey and a pivotal part of the development process. However, it is paramount that we vet them against the Word of God and the calling He has for our life. If we do not thoroughly seek the Lord's wisdom, and we instead jump at all these different types of opportunities, we will find ourselves jumping from thing to thing. It will leave us spinning out of control and not advancing ourselves, or the Kingdom. The Bible says that a double-minded person is unstable in all their ways, being cast to and fro like a wave on the ocean (James 1:6–8).

You can therefore see that the enemy does not play fair when it comes to your destiny. He will persuade you to trade a bad situation for a worse one. It may not seem like that in the beginning, but remember, he comes to steal, kill, and destroy your life (John 10:10). The devil is a liar and his sole purpose is to destroy you and everyone around you. He desperately wants to stop you from fulfilling your destiny, because once again, this gives you power to defeat the principalities and rulers of this world.

Be wary though, for our enemy is very cunning and a master strategist. He will not use only the bad situations in our life to try to derail us, but he will also just as readily materialize in the good times. The Bible says he masquerades as an angel of light (2 Corinthians 11:14).

The scenario may play out something like this: you're traveling along in your journey, doing quite well. Your spouse is happy, the kids are well, and the job is fantastic. You're attending church every Sunday, and you are even tithing. *Man, life is good,* you think to yourself. All of a sudden, out of the blue, an opportunity presents itself for you to achieve something bigger, something higher, something better. Usually this will come in the form of more money, position, or power. Again I believe God does present us with opportunities to do bigger and greater things than we could ever imagine or even believe for ourselves. I believe that is actually part of destiny. But, this is why it is imperative to submit these things to leadership, and more importantly, to God, to ensure it is in alignment with His vision for our life. It is easy to accept the right opportunity but at the wrong time.

In the development process in the Kingdom of God, timing is

a key element. As noted previously, you cannot stay in the chemical solution too long, or you become overexposed. Be extracted and leave too early, and you are underdeveloped. Remember, God is the Master Developer and He has perfect timing. He knows exactly when to remove you from each solution so the brilliance of the original picture shines through. The Bible says you are his masterpiece (Ephesians 2:10). This is an amazing truth. God does not make junk and He will apply His perfect timing as the Master Creator to make sure His masterpiece is perfect in all of His intended ways.

A masterpiece takes time to create. If you think about Leonardo da Vinci or Pablo Picasso, two of history's most prolific painters, it sometimes took years to finish their work. Da Vinci carried the famous Mona Lisa around with him for years until he was able to complete this work—his life's masterpiece. In the same way, the Lord will take His time with you to ensure His masterpiece is complete.

This is why the enemy will expend so many resources to disrupt God's timing in your life. He has found it an effective strategy to present God's intended opportunity, not at the intended time, but at a moment too early in the development process, so it then becomes destructive, rather than constructive. The Bible supports this concept as Paul tells Timothy that they do not put young Christians in positions of authority too soon (1 Timothy 3:6). In all likelihood, this is because they are not fully developed, and therefore they are not strong enough to carry the mantle the opportunity brings with it. It does not suffice to say the timing has anything to do with age. Clearly Timothy was quite young when he was leading a church of fifty thousand people. It was more so a reference to where they were in their development process. Again, if they are taken out too soon they will be underdeveloped and not able to withstand the weight of the pressures that come with that part of the journey.

We can see the same principle at work in basic concepts such as developing body strength. I like to work out on a regular basis, but I did not just one day pick up a three-hundred-pound weight and begin to bench press with ease. It takes time to develop the muscular power needed to be strong enough to carry that weight. We can also apply this same concept as we study our story of Joseph a little deeper.

A presumably beautiful woman with her heart intent on seducing Joseph would have been an opportunity for distraction from his destiny, pulling him out much too soon. During his time as head of Potiphar's household and staff, his daily regiment was most likely incredibly arduous. The enemy, wanting at the very least to steal his destiny from him, to kill him and to destroy him, tried to appeal to the part of him that would desire a woman. An unmarried, celibate man carrying out tasks heavy laden with stress—an attractive woman was the perfect enticement for Joseph to detour him from his pursuit of destiny. But Joseph persevered and resolved to push through, even though standing up for his beliefs and maintaining his integrity meant an even darker room—prison.

Further along in Joseph's story, we see a strong example of the right timing of God. As Joseph's journey began, God gave him dreams that foretold his destiny. He conveyed those dreams at the wrong time to his family and was therefore thrown into the pit, into slavery, and ultimately into prison. Eventually, along came his two new cellmates. At this time, he was governing the whole prison. The Master Developer had caused all things to work together for good in his life, and Joseph had been faithful in walking through his development process. God had used every situation and circumstance to train him up for such a time as this.

Joseph had learned the structure of organizations, human resource practices, and how to manage large institutions. He also learned the crucial practice of hearing God's voice at the right time. This led to the interpretation of the dreams of his new cellmates and eventually the interpretation of the king's dream. At the right time he was able to carry the full weight of the mantle bestowed on him. His whole life had been a development process, preparing him for this mantle. This led him to the fulfillment of his destiny, the saving of not only the nation of Israel but the nation of Egypt and many of the surrounding countries.

This is a powerful story of God's timing and what the fulfillment of destiny can accomplish. God will provide you with discernment when determining His timing in all situations. I believe God has a plan and a purpose, in His perfect time, for your life—a destiny that will change this world. Be determined from this point forward to persevere, push on, and push through! It will be an experience beyond your wildest imaginings!

CHAPTER 4

From Everest to Africa

"THE CLOSEST WE WILL EVER GET TO HEAVEN WHILE STANDING on earth"—this is how people have described Mount Everest. Located in the Himalayas on the border of Nepal and China, it stands at a towering 8,850 meters above sea level. This makes it the largest mountain in the entire world.

Very few people have ever attempted to summit Mount Everest and far fewer have actually accomplished this amazing feat. Extensive physical and mental preparations, along with the proper equipment, are essential before even attempting to make this journey. This is a challenge you cannot undertake on your own. It requires an entire team of skilled experts, including the indispensable local Tibetan guides, to conquer this mammoth mountain. This journey is so immense, the mountain so huge, that it cannot be scaled in a single day even if you climbed for twenty-four hours nonstop.

To make the trek a little more feasible, four different camps, or destination points, have been established along the way to the summit. Each camp serves a different purpose in the fulfillment of the team's journey to the pinnacle of Everest. There are no shortcuts to reach the top. You must pass through all the camps to reach the summit.

Like climbing a mountain, going through the development process is far from easy. At times it can be very painful and even seemingly impossible. As the old saying goes, if it were easy everybody would do it. Unfortunately, like reaching the summit of Everest, very few people try and even fewer succeed in walking in the fullness of their destiny.

The amazing thing about our God is that He accepts us for this journey just as we are. You do not have to be in world-class shape, be overflowing with amazing attributes, or even be a renowned expert on any particular subject matter. All you need to do is say yes to Him, and He will personally guide you through this amazing journey. Getting to the pinnacle of your destiny won't be easy, but it will be worth it for you and for the Kingdom of God. It will take mental preparation, physical willingness, and most imperatively, you must trust your Guide and allow Him to equip you. The fortunate part for us as Christians is that God has given us everything we need for our journey to the summit. He has provided the equipment, skilled team members, an expert guide in the Holy Spirit, and Jesus, who will bear our load if only we ask.

The obedience God requires with that *yes* to Him is for you to be brave enough to take the first step of your journey, even if it means doing it scared.

I'm reminded of a dream that an evangelist friend of mine, Kevin Greer, shared with me. In the dream, a closed door stood in front of Kevin. Jesus walked up to the door, opened it and asked Kevin to go through it. Kevin obeyed and took the steps that Jesus requested. Turning back to look at the door through which he had just walked, he saw that the door frame itself had shrunk down and turned into a key. The key was held out before him, beckoning him to take it. He could not understand why he needed this key because he had just come through the door that the Lord had already opened. However, he did take the key, and once he turned back around and began to walk forward in his journey, he came upon a large wooden door about twenty feet tall. This door was locked up tight. He tried the key that the previous doorframe had created, and it unlocked the door. He then opened the door and walked through it, and as he turned around, that doorframe too, melded into another key. This key then worked on the next locked door. This happened at the next door, and the next door, and then the dream began to speed up. Faster and faster they came, doors and keys, doors and keys. Watching Kevin today, I can say he has indeed walked through many doors on the way to the fulfillment of his destiny.

What I love about the dream is that he needed to walk through the first door to receive the key for the next one. His trust in the Lord and his obedience allowed him to take the first step across the threshold of that first door. The experience he gained from going through that door was the key to open the next door. This is a profound truth. Like the strategically placed camps on Everest, there will be many destination points, or doors, that we must walk through in order to get to the next point in our development process. This is significant in understanding the whole process. Our Guide will lead us through one door at a time to allow each experience to develop us further and put the needed keys in our hand, one after the other.

The typical Everest expedition requires over twenty pounds of equipment and supplies to summit the mountain, and even this is only half the weight of the original expeditions! Often local Tibetans who have climbed the mountain many times previously, are specifically hired both as expert guides and to carry the gear. These experts provide first-time climbers with the best routes and warn them of any impending dangers. With the expert guides carrying the heavy load, new climbers can save their strength and energy for the battle against the elements that will come as they challenge the summit.

In Ephesians 6, God has laid out the entire equipment list necessary for your journey through the development process—the armor of God. The first piece, and arguably one of the most important, is the helmet of salvation. We are to put on the helmet of salvation for the renewing of our mind, allowing it to be transformed into the mind of Christ, which will empower us to conform to the image of Christ. Joyce Meyer's book *The Battlefield of the Mind*[4] clearly explains that your battle will be won or lost in the six inches between your ears. Often the enemy will insert thoughts into your mind to try to distract you or even make you count yourself out of the battle. This is why it is critical to always look back to what the word of God says about who you are in Christ, and declare His truth over your life. That is also why girding your loins everyday with the belt of truth, the second piece of armor, is so incredibly important.

The third piece of God's armor is the breastplate of righteousness. The breastplate of righteousness provides protection for your heart from the attack of the enemy, keeping it soft and malleable before the Lord. One of the most common tactics the enemy will use to attack our heart is offense. He will attempt to use people in your life to cause offense to derail you from moving forward on your journey. If he can keep you looking back, he can stop you from moving forward. Forgiveness and letting go are key in moving on in your journey.

The next to consider are the gospel shoes of peace. They are critical in carrying us along our journey. The power of the gospel is the center of the word of God and should never be forgotten. It is the blood of Jesus, the grace of God, and the empowerment of the Spirit that will allow us to continue to push on through our journey. The gospel shoes of peace allow us to stand firm in the love that Christ has for us. Romans 8:38 says that nothing can separate us from His love. This assurance of His never-failing, unending love fills every part of us with peace.

The shield of faith is the final piece of defensive armor. The Bible is clear that the shield is used to quench the fiery darts of the enemy. It is not only inevitable, it is promised that the enemy will try to attack us while we are pushing through to our destiny; after all, it is his kingdom we are taking. Therefore, having the shield of faith to protect us is a critical element. Fiery darts can take many shapes and forms and the enemy will constantly bombard you with these attacks throughout each and every day. Ranging from harmful thoughts being placed in your mind, to physical assaults perpetrated by pawns of the enemy, these attacks can be severely detrimental to your godly pursuits. Having our faith placed firmly in believing that Jesus Christ is who He says He is, and will do all that He has promised to do, is the only way we are truly protected, enabling us to stand strong in all we do.

The concept of this shield reminds me of the battle scenes we've all witnessed in medieval movies. The attacking archers would set fire to their arrow tips, pull back their bows by the hundreds, and launch their burning arrows at the opposing army. To defend against this onslaught, the entire army would raise their shields above their heads to form a protective barrier that guarded them against the incoming assault. It provided a solid protection against the fiery arrows. So stand up with the shield of faith and defend yourself.

Finally, the last piece of our armor and the only offensive piece is the sword of the Spirit—the mighty and holy Word of God. As Jesus was in the wilderness being tempted by the devil, every response He gave was, "It is written!" (Matthew 4 KJV). The word of God is more powerful than any two-edged sword (Hebrews 4:12) and should be used on a regular basis throughout your journey. The enemy cannot withstand its power and it will provide you victory in every circumstance. The Word of God should also be used to vet your destiny. Your destiny should line up with what is written in God's word. If it does not seem to do so, pray and seek God for a clear revelation of your destiny. Though we cannot expect a literal declaration that provides you with a step-by-step instruction manual of what you are to do, it is the alignment of principles we must seek.

If you find the vision of your destiny still hazy at this point, keep reading. It is my intent to give you a more complete understanding of your personal calling in the body of Christ. Remember, in His Word, Jesus gave all of us the great commission, which is the ultimate fulfillment of our destiny as the body of Christ—becoming His bride. Your personal destiny will absolutely be found in Him. The sword of the Spirit, the Word of God, is therefore a key part of our armor.

The Bible is clear that this armor is to be put on every day because we have an enemy of our destiny, and every day will be a battle as you push forward into it. This may seem overwhelming to you, but remember we are not alone. As you push on you will become stronger, and the battle will be less fatiguing. It will even become enjoyable! It is a great joy to take ground from the enemy and set captives free, especially in areas of our own weaknesses or challenges.

DEVELOPMENTAL KEY 2: Perseverance

One of my biggest battles on my journey is that I am visually impaired—to the point that I am considered blind. Blindness has been an extremely difficult personal battle that I choose to overcome every single day. Perseverance is a developmental key that I cannot neglect.

My battle with blindness is like going through slow and agonizing torture. I have a genetic retinal condition that guarantees me I will eventually go completely blind. The deterioration of my sight happens extremely slowly over time. It's like being in a room where the light is on a dimmer switch being slowly turning down bit by bit, but your eyes do not adjust. It just gets harder and harder to see. The worst part at this point is that it is currently incurable, and there's nothing I can do to stop that light from being turned down and eventually off. It's like being in a roller coaster car and hearing the click, click, click as the cars ascend to the top of the ride and you know what's about to happen, but no matter what you do you can't get off the ride. I have tried everything I can to fight back against this horrible disease. Physically, I have tried almost every natural remedy on the planet. I take multiple vitamins and supplements. I have also gone to many different doctors. In the spiritual, I have sought prayer from dozens of people, and I pray for my eyes on a daily basis. From a theological position, I know that my eyes are healed, and it is just a matter of time before the healing will manifest itself. My reality right now, though, is that I still have a visual impairment; it is a fact that I have to push through daily. One thing that I have done throughout this battle is not to allow my disability to define who I am. I allow Christ and the Word of God to define that. I am more than a conqueror. I am the head and not the tail. I am going above, and I refuse to go beneath!

Once, I was conversing with God while out running by myself. I asked Him, "Why do I need to pray and ask for healing? Why don't You just do it?" These very raw and honest conversations with God are not only good, but are extremely necessary. He's a big God and

He can take it. The Holy Spirit spoke to me very clearly that day and said, "Jeff, Jesus has not held anything back from you. When Christ was beaten and then died on the cross, shedding His blood for you, it was finished. He is not holding back your healing. Rather, you need to contend for it from the enemy, walking out of the victory that Christ has already paid for through the breaking of His body and His shed blood on the cross." This was nothing short of a revelation for me. It empowered me to press forward in the battle for my eyesight. We are in a battle and as we fight, we are taking ground back from the enemy.

As you can probably imagine, this is a huge battle—mentally, physically, and emotionally. It is something that I have to push through on a daily basis. To succeed in this, I must continually put on the whole armor of God. I live daily what I write to you. Each piece empowers me in this fight. Without revisiting them all, I will encapsulate how they apply in my life. The helmet allows me to continue to renew my mind and fight back against the thoughts that tell me I am not worthy, that I am broken, and that I can't do what God has called me to do. I speak the truth of who I am in Christ! The breastplate helps me to protect my heart even from things I don't understand, like why my healing has not yet manifested. I know that God is good no matter the circumstance; some days are just harder for me than others. The shoes of the gospel of peace give me assurance in knowing that Jesus has paid the price for my salvation and healing and that it is only a matter of time before it'll manifest itself, either through a miraculous healing or scientific breakthrough. I believe God uses all manner of wisdom in the restoration of his people. The shield allows me to have faith in the gospel to know that what He says is true and that He is not a man that He should lie. I know that I am fighting from a position of strength at the right hand of the Father. Finally, I use the sword of the Spirit daily to battle the enemy and, most importantly, to help me pray without ceasing. Though I do not literally pray twenty-four hours a day, my lifestyle is a prayer. I may not be perfect, but I try my best to yield myself to Him daily. The difference between a winner and a loser, as I always tell my children, is that if a winner were knocked down one hundred times, they would get up one hundred and one times. The only way you can lose is to quit—don't do it. Do not be defined by your defeats, but put on your armor, and be empowered by your victories.

Now that you have the context from which to view this let's travel to Africa to witness the mission trip that became a very significant event in my life. But first, let's look at how God intricately set the stage, placing specific destination points along my path to lead me to, and prepare me for Africa. Three years before this mission trip, I had a dream that I was in an African village that was overrun with garbage. I was preaching, and the power of God hit so strongly that people were knocked backward. Then in my dream, I saw the continent of Africa washed in blood, north to south, and east to west. This dream was parallel to a vision given to Reinhard Bonnke. From there, three weeks before I was scheduled to go to Uganda, I was invited to the Reinhard Bonnke School of Evangelism and received a powerful ministry impartation as God connected me with Todd White, Daniel Kolenda and Reinhard Bonnke. God had prepared me for what I would face in Africa.

The ministry team I was with was in the country of Uganda in the city of Kampala. The district was called Luzira. The crusade was taking place on a flat, dirt plain that had been packed down from hundreds of years of foot traffic. The red African dirt sticks to everything, especially your shoes. The platform for the stage was covered by a large metal roof, supported by four metal poles. To the east of us were various shops with vendors selling their wares. To the left of the platform was a hill that went up about thirty feet. On the top of this hill were businesses—notorious ones. There was a gentleman's club, a gambling house, and a bar. To the right and behind the platform was a flat piece of land buried in garbage. Nestled in amongst the garbage were small one and two-room shacks. It was here that one could find the slums of Kampala.

Some homes were held up by solid wood walls, but others were just slat walls with dilapidated roofs. A putrid smell from all the garbage on the ground filled the air. The stench would be reminiscent of a long neglected trash can finally being opened. The burning of the garbage only slightly masked the strong odor. It was not uncommon to see kids playing in the trash heap, despite the unappealing atmosphere. It pulled on my heart.

When I first walked onto the field by the platform, approximately a dozen small African children swarmed me within seconds. They were touching and petting the hair on my arms. I love the African people. They are so warm and inviting to outsiders. I tried to make the little ones feel welcome and even played games with them. Some children would just come up to me and hold my hand as I walked around. In some ways it brought me back to my own childhood. I too, grew up in a very poor home void of all luxuries and even some necessities. For me to see this kind of poverty was overwhelming, especially knowing in my heart that even if I gave all I had, I couldn't change anything. That evening, as the meeting went on, many people gave their lives to Jesus, but I could not shake the image of the children in the garbage.

That night after the first meeting, we left the field and drove approximately three blocks where we pulled into a compound. This compound contained a Western-style mall that had a Kentucky Fried Chicken. The contrast to where we just were, was startling. It was like we drove across the world in only three blocks. While sitting down to eat chicken, I began to ask questions about the locals. I learned that two-thirds of the city lived in extreme poverty. The reality of this in practical terms meant they only ate one meal of squashed up corn every day or two. I began to feel a sense of hopelessness coming over me. It was the helpless feeling of not being able to do anything for these people in any practical way. While this tidal wave of emotions washed over me, I was eating crisp, hot Kentucky Fried Chicken. I put the chicken down. I could not eat anymore, as the feeling in my gut was overtaking me. It was more than I could bear.

That night, Face timing with my wife in my hotel room, she immediately knew that something was wrong. I was very downtrodden, not myself at all. The enemy had taken hold of me and shoved me into a very dark place. I began to nitpick about the team and began musing as to why I was even there. "Why do they want a blind guy that they have to lead around from place to place?" I asked. I have my peripheral vision so I can walk during the day, but at night I am completely blind. The voice in my head was telling me I was just a liability, of no value to the team. I said to her, "If they want my money, I could just write a check and go home." I even went so far as to consider catching the very next available flight back home. My wife, being the amazing woman of God she is, suggested that I get a good night's sleep and look at it with fresh eyes in the morning.

I heeded her advice, and revelation dawned with the sun. The enemy was trying to overcome me with darkness and hopelessness. If he could get me to go home, he could stop me from taking the next step in my destiny. I literally got down on my knees in the hotel room and began to pray. I said, "God, please forgive me for my lack of faith. I'll do whatever you want me to do here. I submit myself to you. Please just use me today in any way that you can." I immediately felt that heaviness lift from me, and hope began to flood in. I had a revelation about the power of the gospel and realized that these people did not need my money; they needed a Savior. That part would change their lives, and with that part, I could help them. It was an incredible, refreshing feeling. The Bible says, "Hope deferred makes the heart sick" (Proverbs 13:12 NLT). At that moment I realized that hope restored brings new life.

That night after a time of prayer, we headed back to the field where the meeting was held. I spent the majority of the evening simply standing beside the platform interceding. Near the end, my pastor, Joel Wells, had an altar call, first for salvation, and then for healing. Many, many people came forward. As I stood beside the stage with my hand on the metal support beam of the platform, I suddenly felt a small hand go over top of mine. It was a young African girl. I know now she was five years old. I put my hand on top of hers and then she put her hand on top of my other hand and used me to guide herself around the pole that held the metal roof structure of the platform. I don't know why I did this, but once she was in front of me, I placed her two hands in a prayer position and began to bless her. After about a minute of this, I began to walk among the crowd. Hindered by my eyesight, I could not venture deep, but stayed within about a fifteen-foot parameter of light availed to me by the stage lights. I prayed for a few adults, but I felt nothing. I believe this was because that is not where the Lord wanted me at that moment. Walking back to the stage, I heard the Holy Spirit whisper, "Do not suffer the children to come unto Me." When I reached the stage, a small hand, that of the same little girl, grabbed mine and pushed it to another little girl, who was leaning against the stage watching the band play. I know now this was the little girl's seven-year-old sister. Instinctively, I knew she wanted me to pray for her. I placed my hand on her shoulder and began to pray. I heard the Holy Spirit tell me to place my hands on her ears and pray for them. I was obedient to His voice and did so. As I did, I felt the power of God moving. After I had prayed, I started back to the stage, feeling like I was done for the night. All of a sudden, the five-year-old girl grabbed my hand, and pulled me down to the ground where she was now sitting. In my peripheral vision, I could see her looking up at me. She was centered in the middle of a large light, and she glowed almost like a little angel. She said, "My eyes don't see properly." Understandably, these words were enough to shatter me into a million pieces right on the spot. I don't know how, other than God, but somehow I did not shatter. Instead, something rose up from inside of me, and I placed my hand over her eyes.

In my mind I was crying out to God saying, *I can't do this! I can't believe this is happening!* But out of my mouth came different words. I heard myself saying, "Sweetheart, in the Bible it says that Jesus has healed many blind people, and I believe that He can heal you too." I could feel her eyelids fluttering under my hand. I took my hand off her eyes, and I asked her if she could see. She looked around, and she lit up like a million-watt light bulb. She shouted, "I can see properly!" I instantly burst into tears and began to sob uncontrollably. She then grabbed my hand and began to point to the water bottle on the stage. I thought she wanted a drink. I called over a local lady, and she spoke to her in their native language. The little girl told the lady that when she looked at things, it was like looking through water. When I prayed for her, she saw two things fall off her eyes and she now could see properly! While this was happening, the seven-year-old girl came over with another lady. She said she'd had a problem with her ears and could not hear well, and when I was praying for her, she felt a knock and then a pop in her ears. Now she can hear properly. The miracles were documented and the girls' mother came the next night and verified them. Glory to God!

It was amazing to me how straightforward it all was. It did not take hours of prayer or anything of the like. It was simply the power of the Holy Spirit working through a yielded, obedient person who was determined to walk into his destiny. The Bible says that God is strong in our weakness (2 Corinthians 12:10), and of this I am living proof. He used my weakness to show His strength. The words of Pastor Joel from his sermon on July 17, 2016, tell another part of the story from his perspective and its profound impact on my life and the lives of others:

> "In a couple of months, I will be leading a team of eighteen people from this church to Uganda to preach in gospel and business forums. I can promise you that fear and doubt are already beginning to attack the minds of the team members including myself.
>
> "Last year, I took Jeff on the trip. A few days into the trip, Jeff almost booked his plane ticket home—that is God's honest truth—because there was a fear that was raging inside of him that he had nothing to offer. By the grace of God, he pushed through his fear. He ended up speaking at a small men's breakfast that had several local businessmen attending. As he told his story of what God had done in his life and the business that God has blessed him with, these businessmen began to pump him with questions. This led to further discussions and ultimately

to some business ventures in Kampala, and a vision birthed to return a year later with a team of businessmen to impact the community and business leaders. The team of eighteen people traveling over and the expanded vision for this year is a direct result of that men's breakfast at the end of the trip.

"On top of that, Jeff has gotten involved with Leadership Impact in our community. Doors have begun to open to speak in different places in Canada and around the world for him. You see, Jeff has discovered that before he was even born, God called him. Fear wanted to destroy and derail God's destiny for his life. But I can tell you that I am excited watching him stretch his wings and push forward as he is growing in his understanding that God is with Him and that God has called him for this. He has said to me a number of times, 'I think I have found my calling.'

"Yes, you have."[5]

When he invited me to go with him to Africa, Pastor Joel was unaware that he would play such an integral part in my destiny.

So even though I know Mount Everest is massive and the journey strenuous and long, the pinnacle—the summit—will be worth it. This is why even to this day people will risk their very lives to achieve its peak, so that they can stand on top of the world! The amazing thing for us is that our destiny, our calling, will take us much, much higher, even higher than the top of the world! It may even take you around the world. Let your journey begin this very day! My hopes and my prayers are that this book will provide the spark, the inspiration, and the tools you need to set you well on your way. Even if it means doing it scared, take that first step! But do not be afraid, for you will not be alone because destiny definitely is a team sport!

CHAPTER 5

Destiny Is a Team Sport

IN ALL AREAS OF LIFE, SUCCESS REQUIRES SUFFICIENT PREPARAtion. If we don't make adequate preparations, we find ourselves lacking in some capacity, and we certainly would not be able to achieve any standard of excellence. This is also true as we set out along the path of our destiny.

God our Father, the Master Developer, will never send us on a journey ill-equipped. On the contrary, He gives us the best of the best. He gives us His very power, His Holy Spirit, as our guide. The Holy Spirit is a critical component to the success of achieving our life summit—our destiny. It is so critical, in fact, that as part of the salvation plan, Jesus was willing to lay down His very life so that the Holy Spirit would be released on the earth (John 16:7). Paul reminds us that God has even placed the Holy Spirit in our hearts as a deposit that guarantees everything He has promised us (2 Corinthians 1:22). And the Holy Spirit Himself does not come empty handed. He comes bearing gifts from our Father (1 Corinthians 12:11). These gifts empower us each in various ways to fulfill our diverse roles in the body of Christ. By connecting with the Holy Spirit, the power of God, we are equipped to do all things through Christ who is our strength (Philippians 4:13). This is why it is so important to heed His guidance.

In *The Prophetic Team Workbook*,[6] Diane Harrison teaches that we are created to hear the voice of God, but learning to recognize that voice is a process. Our confidence grows as we practice listening and receive some form of confirmation that *yes*, we are hearing from the

Lord. As the Master Guide, the voice of the Holy Spirit will come to us in different ways. It will take different shapes and forms at specific times in our life. That is why it is so crucial to practice being in His presence and taking the time to learn and to listen to that still small voice. In some situations, that still small voice can mean the difference between tragedy and triumph.

Unfortunately, many people do not heed His voice and do not take the time to practice being in His presence. This almost always leads to some form of tragedy. This being said the question becomes, "How can I hear the voice of the Holy Spirit?" The best description I have ever heard of the practice of His presence is that the Holy Spirit is like a radio station that is always transmitting, always wanting to speak to you, and all we need to do is to take the time and dial in to the right frequency.

The Holy Spirit does not, however, exclusively work in the whispers in your heart. On the contrary, He will speak to us through the Word of God, through prophetic words, images, dreams, songs, and impressions. We can even receive revelation through our five physical senses. We sometimes hear His voice through His creation of the world around us, and very often through the people God has put in our lives. Our Father, as a Master Developer, is a unifier, and He will cause all things to work together for our good (Romans 8:28). In other words, He will cause all situations to speak to us while weaving them into the mosaic of our life, which encompasses our destiny, as long as we are tuned in to listen.

As we journey into knowing how the Holy Spirit operates, please note that I am not referring to Old Testament epiphanies where He appeared outwardly and spoke to people as an angel of God, but rather, how He speaks to our hearts. The Holy Spirit has been speaking to the hearts of men for generations, and I believe this is one of the primary ways He speaks to us today.

To understand this concept, let's look a little deeper into how we are designed as human beings. We have a soul, which is our mind, will, and emotions, and we live in a physical body. But, we are a three-part being; we are also spirit, which is referenced biblically as the heart of man. Therefore, the Holy Spirit speaks to our spirit and then we, in turn, hear it in our mind. This is often why when you hear the Holy Spirit talking, it can sound like your own voice.

This is incredibly confusing for most people and where I find that many stumble in hearing the voice of God. A major part of this confusion is that there is more than one source for the voice in our head, and they all sound similar. The challenge is to figure out from where that voice is coming.

The three voices we hear are the Holy Spirit, our own soul, and Satan. This is why I strongly contend that believing the entire Bible is so critical. The Holy Spirit will never speak anything that is contrary to the Word of God. The enemy of our destiny, however, will do just that, warping and twisting the truth until it is out of alignment with God's Word, which can then bring about disastrous results. This is a secure way to measure and discern the source of the voice.

Remember, the Bible says to study and show yourself approved (2 Timothy 2:15). I believe an extensive part of this is putting the Word of God in context, thus divulging the whole meaning of the scripture and not allowing for fragmented half-truths. Many times I have seen people take one verse or even part of the verse and build an entire doctrine on it. With that statement, I'm not looking to get sidetracked by doctrinal issues; for as Paul said, "Don't get involved in foolish, ignorant arguments" (2 Timothy 2:23 NLT). I am solely interested in helping people avoid getting diverted and helping them to learn to hear the voice of God more clearly.

Another way to train yourself to hear the voice of the Holy Spirit is to read one of the many informative books available on hearing God speak and on prophecy and interpretation. It is also important to surround yourself with spiritual leaders, whom you trust, and seek a multitude of counselors as you are seeking God's voice in different situations. This will help you distinguish your own desires—your own voice—from that of the Lord's. Overall, the key is to practice being in His presence by spending time with Him and steadfastly tuning in to the right frequency. This will empower you onward and upward to achieving your destiny.

DEVELOPMENTAL KEY 3: Unity

Along with speaking to our hearts, another facet of the Holy Spirit is to unify us with our partners in destiny—our expedition team—to form the body of Christ. People come from all over the world to tackle Mount Everest, which means the Sherpa guides do not speak the language of most of its climbers. That is why the ability to learn how to communicate with them and with each other is crucial. As the body of Christ, we are all from different parts of the world. We are from different tribes and nations, and therefore, we all speak different languages. But we are all united through God's Holy Spirit. We have a common goal because of the common guide, the Holy Spirit. He is the unifier. He ties everything together and unites us as we learn to hear His voice.

This body of Christ is the fullness of the original image, which makes it imperative for you to interconnect with others in unity when walking out your destiny. This pinpoints the third developmental key to unlocking your potential—unity.

Like summiting Mount Everest, we are only able to achieve this unity as we fulfill our calling in Jesus as a unified body. This unity of destiny, I believe, is one of the most powerful forces in the universe, and this is exactly why the enemy is so set on destroying it.

Much like the expedition team that is required to climb Mount Everest, there are different parts of the body of Christ. In 1 Corinthians 12:12–27, Paul extensively compares our physical body with its specific parts, to the different roles in the body of Christ. He identifies that our bodies have many parts, and God has put each part just where He wants it. It is the same in the body of Christ. We all serve a different critical function when we apply the spiritual gifts that the Holy Spirit has given us. This is why it is imperative that we discover what our calling is and connect with the incredible power found in our destiny. Once we can do this, we can begin to build the living temple, serving in unity, as God desires.

But this does not come without much opposition. Mark 3:25 says a house divided cannot stand, and that's exactly what the enemy wants: to divide the house. I believe this is why Satan himself has set out to accomplish this very task. The house refers to the body of Christ; the one in which Christ Himself is the chief cornerstone. Each individual in this body is a living stone held together by the word of God and the love of Christ. This being the case, God will put many structures and relationships into place in our lives to mold and shape the living stones into what He wills them to be.

I believe that marriage and family are such institutions designed by God to play a primary role in this plan for our development. They help us develop Christ's love, and smooth out the rough edges of the living stones so that we may connect together. Looking at today's society, this would explain why marriage and the family are so greatly under attack.

God has purposefully designed marriage, and subsequently the family, as an integral part in the fulfillment of the Kingdom expansion. The Bible is clear that it is not good that man be alone (Genesis 2:18). It goes on to say that the man shall leave his parents, cleave to his wife, and the two shall become one (Genesis 2:24). Matthew 18:20 ensures us that where two or three are gathered together in His name, there He is in the midst of them. In Matthew 18:19, Jesus teaches that if two agree on earth concerning anything they ask, it will be done for them by His Father in heaven. Those are all nation shaking, world-changing promises. To further expand on the importance of unity in our marriage, family, and the body of Christ, the last prayer that Jesus prayed on this earth was that we would come together in unity (John 17:11).

The current distractions of doctrine, worship styles, and other trivial factors have fractured the church and kept us from uniting under the one thing that is important: Jesus and the destiny He has for His church, the bride. Jesus' words to Peter in Matthew 16:18 can be applied to the whole body of Christ: "Upon this rock I will build my church, and all the powers of hell will not conquer it" (NLT). I strongly believe that unity is a key in the final defeat of our enemy and actualizing the victory that Christ has won on the cross. I have experienced this first hand.

Walking in Unity

Recently my wife and I had an opportunity to speak at a high school for a chapel service. I have spoken on my own before, and God, through his faithfulness, has done some really powerful things. This, however, would be the first time that my wife and I would unite together and speak as a couple.

My wife and I were married for only about thirty days before we got pregnant for the first time. This was an amazing blessing and I would not have changed it. However, the timing of this child did not facilitate any honeymoon stage for our marriage whatsoever. I believe the honeymoon stage is a critical time in a marriage, as it gives the opportunity to learn about each other's quirks and how to live with each other, prior to introducing the dynamic of children. The first five years of our marriage were very dark. I was a selfish, insecure little boy, who had been hurt by his upbringing. This, coupled with my limbic responses (I will explain limbic responses in detail in chapter 7), caused the first five years to be a very difficult period, filled with fighting, yelling, and all their terrible repercussions. I had thought that by getting married, all of my problems would go away. I believed that my wife was simply there to make me happy. But that is not the truth we find in the Bible. On top of this, during these dark days I also began my business, which only added more tension and stress to our home.

When you come into a marriage, no matter who you are, you bring baggage. I brought a whole tractor-trailer full of baggage and this caused many of our issues. My wife, as amazing as she is, wasn't perfect either. Although she came from a good Christian home, she still had luggage. It was just different from mine; not to mention much prettier!

It took us many years and many tears, tools, and loving support from family and friends to walk through the sorting out of this baggage. I have failed her many times and in countless ways, but she has always shown me the grace and the love of Christ.

By the measurement of the world today, we should not still be married, but God saw this differently. He caused all things to work together for good in our marriage. It has been a very challenging road, but one that was worth traveling. I would choose to do it all over again in a heartbeat. I feel that I am married to the most wonderful woman in the world today, and I'm not just saying that for the purpose of this book. God knew exactly what I needed in a life-mate—in a partner on my journey to the summit—and this is all found in my wife.

In the beginning of our marriage, I was looking at the negative, although God did give me glimpses of that end picture. Now I am seeing our Father developing her, and I see the beauty of that final photograph coming out every day. She's amazing in ways that I cannot even express, and I love her dearly. I know I am gushing, but she does deserve it. So the fact that we were now here, over a decade into our marriage, in love with each other and finally being able to step into ministry together, was a powerful time in our life; one that the enemy did not want to see happen.

Almost instantly after the Lord confirmed that we should be speaking together, the attacks began. Whispers came to her mind, casting doubt and bringing condemnation. The voice was saying she was not good enough and she had nothing to bring to the table, both of which were lies from the pit of hell. I believe that my wife has a calling and an anointing on her life to see women of all ages set free from the bonds this world has put on them, such bonds as performance issues and fabricated beauty that encourages a false identity.

Although my wife didn't come from a terrible background like I did, she has an extremely powerful testimony of what the Lord has done in her life. She grew up in a small Christian town on the prairies in Canada. Her family, on both sides, was Christian, going back at least one or two generations. She was born to two wonderful parents in covenant and into that blessing, but she still had to walk out her own life's journey. She has had many challenges along the way that she has been able to overcome. She had something powerful to say to these young, impressionable people, and the enemy did not want that to happen.

Three days before we were supposed to speak, I became extremely sick. I experienced severe abdominal pain, I could not get out of bed, and my body was wracked with fever. We were afraid it was appendicitis. After a full day of this, I decided to see the doctor the next morning. The doctor performed the examination and ruled out my appendix and said I would recover on my own, but she ordered a routine x-ray just to ensure there were no other problems. It was in that x-ray that they found it: a large mass in my abdomen.

I had to wait until the next day for the results. It was one of those dreaded phone calls in which the doctor wants to see you, but they will not tell you anything of significance until you are in the office with the doctor. It was here she informed me of the mass in my gut and the need to do an emergency ultrasound. She said it had formed quickly and it could be very dangerous, as it was pushing on my intestines. I have since learned, and can now highly recommend to you, that if you are in a similar situation, do NOT Google your condition. You will only find out you're definitely going to die from cancer, and the resulting stress just exasperates the situation.

I went home, walked upstairs to our bedroom, into the master bathroom and released the flood of tears warranted by this circumstance. With the tears came a crying out to God, emphatically expressing I did not want to die. It's not that I didn't want to go to heaven, I just did not want to leave my wife and kids behind, having to struggle through the debilitating pain my death would ultimately cause. The pain in my gut was one of the worst I've ever felt in my life. But it wasn't from the mass; it was from the sense of loss of what should have been and what I would miss in my kids' lives. Flashes of missed weddings and grandchildren rolled through my mind as I cried before the Lord.

That night, still very sick, I was lying in bed watching a show on my phone, when there was a prayer time for healing on the show. I remember a man named Pat praying, and he said somebody had a blocked colon and that God was healing it right then. I felt an incredible heat come over my body. I thought my fever was returning, so I took my temperature. I had no fever, but I was still feeling the heat throughout my body. Peace came over me, and I believed I was healed.

The next morning when I woke up, I felt relaxed, and my body seemed to be working well. My wife and I went to the emergency ultrasound that had been booked for me. The technician slathered me up with the lubrication gel that allows the device to slide over your abdomen. I remember her measuring all different parts of my body. She kept going over the same spots time and time again. I asked her, "What's going wrong? Did you find something?" She assured me not to worry and asked if it was my doctor who told me I had a mass in my abdomen. At the end of the exam, she told me if there was a serious issue they would contact me within an hour or two. If it wasn't serious I would not hear from them for a couple of days.

This ultrasound exam took place on the morning of the day we were supposed to speak to the high school students. We had a decision to make at that point. Do we look at the wind and the waves, or do we push into what we feel God has called us to do? I decided to put my faith in God. Regardless of the results, I was going to serve Him. I would speak. My wife, on the other hand, had decided to back out. She had been under a considerable amount of stress and pressure from everything that was going on. As I was laid out sick in bed, she was busy tending to our home and four children. Understandably, she said she did not feel prepared. All she had to speak from was her rough copy of the notes she had written out to tell her story.

Her decision was difficult for me to accept, because I really felt strongly she was to be there with me as a partner in our destiny, walking out this next step in the process. However, I have learned to let the

Holy Spirit do His perfect work. I walked alongside her and honored her wishes. In the past, I would have given her a lecture about how she was missing what God wanted her to do. That never worked. It only led to us being divided, and the enemy being the winner.

She drove me to the high school and remained in the room. As the worship began, I sat thinking through things and asking God what He wanted me to say, because everything I had prepared was tied in to my wife speaking with me. I began to pray and pray. As I sat there worshiping with my eyes closed, praying to God, I felt a sudden smear across my forehead. I did not know what had just happened. I heard somebody say, "Be blessed," and that was it. They disappeared. It was oil on my forehead. Was I just a victim of a drive-by anointing? All of a sudden, my wife comes and sits beside me and says, "I'm going to do it."

"Going to do what?" I asked.

"I'm going to come up and speak."

To be honest, I was stunned at this point, but delighted that she was obedient to what God was speaking to her. What I did not know was that somebody else prayed for her and this lady, a woman of God, had spoken into her life. This woman of God became a partner with my wife in her development process that day, helping her in the fulfillment of her destiny.

I was soon introduced by the worship leader and went up to the front. Then I invited my wife to come forward. Calling her to the front to speak with me was an amazing moment in my life. It was like I was calling her into the next stage of her development process. I had to fight hard not to cry. I felt the anointing of the Holy Spirit, and I knew this was a critical point in our destiny together.

As we spoke in the chapel, passing the microphone back and forth, the Holy Spirit fell over that place, and it was incredible. There were about one hundred students there that day, and when we asked for a response, which included having them all write down the lie the enemy was speaking to them and throw it in the trash can, almost every single student came forward. There were celebrations happening all around the room, and tears were plentiful. Many people gave their lives and hearts to Jesus.

After the chapel we received a lot of hugs and congratulations, but by far the best part was that for many days afterward, everybody told me how amazing my wife was! She spoke with power and authority, even though she read it just from her rough copy. She was brave, and the Lord used it. One day my hope is that she will write her own account of this event and share how the Lord can use your rough copy too.

Unity between man and wife is a powerful force, and through it, God can do amazing things. But He does not stop with this relationship. Along with spouses and immediate family members, God puts other people on your expedition team to help form you as a living stone. Some members come and go over time, but each one is an important part of your life's journey.

The story of Paul and Barnabas and how they literally changed the world together is a great example of this. You need to have both a Paul and a Barnabas in your life. A *Paul* is typically a mentor who will speak wisdom into your life while keeping you accountable from a position of authority. You cannot have authority unless you have been under authority. The Bible says much in support of this point (Ephesians 1:21–22, Matthew 8:9). But you also need that *Barnabas* who will come alongside you and work in the fields as a peer, encourage you, and keep you accountable as a friend.

Along with these two types of people, you also need a *Timothy*: someone who you are mentoring and pouring into, helping them to fulfill their destiny. And, of course, you need all those sandpaper people, the ones who help you develop all that faithful endurance! Yes, destiny is definitely a team sport. By the way, the ultrasound confirmed that the Lord had, in fact, healed me!

PART TWO

CHAPTER 6

God's Positioning System

When we are headed to a new destination, we do not hesitate to ask for directions, consult a map, or program it into our GPS and carefully follow the given instructions. How much more important is it to follow the directions when the destination point is one along the path to the fulfillment of our destiny? The Holy Spirit is this expert guide in the journey to our life summit—our destiny. It is therefore critical for us to listen to His direction. Not only must we listen, but also we must obey and do just what He asks us to do. And just as important, maybe even more so, is to do what He asks *when* He asks us to do it.

We can compare this to the critical nature of proper timing when using an electronic GPS. Just like a GPS giving the warning of an impending turn that needs to be made or a correction in the path that needs to be taken, The Holy Spirit will provide critical guidance and direction while we traverse our life's journey. Failure to listen and obey GPS instructions can cause you to get lost or to take a wrong turn, making your journey much longer. The same is true of the Holy Spirit. His job is to get you to your destination point as quickly, smoothly, and safely as possible while helping and impacting as many people as possible along the way.

The Holy Spirit is God's GPS—God's Positioning System. He operates in conjunction with the Father and the Son. The timing of the Holy Spirit will line up with the Father's timing to maximize your development. It will also protect you and keep you from falling into any traps set by the enemy to derail you and stop you from developing.

Timing is a critical element in the process when you are developing the final picture. Hebrews 11:1 and 12:2 show that faith is a *now* word. Wait too long and the negative will be overexposed. Do it too quickly or prematurely, and it will be underdeveloped. We can trust in His perfect timing to lead us through our development process, and this kind of obedience requires submission. The challenge is that the spirit is willing, but the flesh is weak.

As laid out in chapter one, this all began in the garden. The Bible says that prior to the fall, there was no shame (Genesis 2:25). When sin ushered in the fall of man, it also brought shame, which separated Adam and Eve from God. They covered themselves with fig leaves and hid from Him (Genesis 3:10). And thus, sin and the subsequent shame became the primary tools the devil uses to separate us from God and His will for our life. They are also the root source of many problems we face in our lives today. The enemy had persuaded Eve to focus on the potential of becoming wise and gaining knowledge. With her fixation on this, she failed to submit to the Father's command. She disobeyed and thus fell into the curse. This brought in sin, shame and condemnation, which is a double-edged sword.

As a result of shame and condemnation, we can feel that God is angry with us. This can make submission difficult or even seemingly impossible. This is especially true for those who have been hurt in the past, either by people close to them or by the church itself. It can also be compounded if the person who inflicted the wound is a father or authority figure. The truth is, we all fall short of the glory of God, and people are not perfect (Romans 3:23). We all come into this world in a fallen state, as negatives. Our families, communities, and the church are comprised of these very people, and therefore are imperfect in themselves. With this being so, we cannot expect to never be offended or hurt. Once you have been hurt badly enough, you can develop trust wounds. If you will not trust, you will find it extremely difficult to submit to anyone, even God. But God is faithful, and He can be trusted. His plans for us are good (Jeremiah 29:11), and He can heal even the deepest of trust wounds. It is in submitting to Him that we open ourselves up to receive all the blessings He has promised us. And He already gave us all we need to accomplish this.

The separation of man from the Creator brought on from the fall in the garden hurt the Father deeply; so much so that in His wisdom, He had put a plan for our redemption in place before the beginning of time. This plan, outlined in Ephesians 1, as noted earlier, was to regain His creation and not only redeem us but to empower us and to give us life and life more abundantly. This is why the deposit of our inheritance, the Holy Spirit, is critical and why we need to heed His guidance.

DEVELOPMENTAL KEY 4: Faith

It is through God's grace that He gave us the Holy Spirit to come alongside and lead us, heal us, and help us to be obedient. The Bible says God has given a measure of faith to every person (Romans 12:3). I believe this initial measure of faith, the fourth developmental key, is what draws you to God. The Bible says without faith it is impossible to please God (Hebrews 11:6). We must believe the Lord is a rewarder of those who diligently seek Him. Choosing to place faith in the Father allows you to have the trust you need to be able to submit to Him. This is contrary to the plan of the enemy. He wants sin, and the shame and condemnation that come with it, to separate you from God and make you fear placing your trust in Him. This fear is paralyzing and will keep you debilitated.

The good news is that God is love, and perfect love casts out all fear (1 John 4:18)! The powerful truth is that submission and obedience to the Holy Spirit give us even more faith, which provides the empowerment and the ability to submit and obey the Father's greater plan. Unfortunately, like the process of development, this is not instant. Faith is like a muscle, and submission and obedience to what God is calling you to do is working it out. The more you submit and obey, the stronger your faith becomes and then the bigger the things will be that the Father calls you to do. It's a cycle that builds you up and up into the fulfillment of your destiny.

This is critically important because the fullness of your destiny is a very heavy mantle to carry and one that takes time to develop the strength to fulfill and bear. If you are willing to take that initial leap of faith, He will cause all things to work together for good in your life, and He will make you the head and not the tail. He'll cause you to stand up, move forward, and be a conqueror!

DEVELOPMENTAL KEY 5: Trust

Everything begins with the trust that enables submission. This is the fifth developmental key. This is a significant one in moving forward in the development process. Trust opens the door and allows the necessary submission and obedience to the Father, which will connect us to His greater plan. The Bible is clear that we are one body of which Christ is the head, and we are to work together (Ephesians 4). As laid out in chapter three, "Destiny is a Team Sport," unity is a key to the Kingdom expansion. We are called to work together to further the Kingdom, and we are all connected in God's plan through unity in the body of Christ.

So submission, the first developmental key introduced, does not just go vertically, it also has to go horizontally. The Bible says submit one to another (Ephesians 5:21). We are not called to live as islands unto ourselves, building our own kingdoms. We are called to serve the Lord and each other, following our guide, the Holy Spirit, and obeying the instructions laid out for us in the Word of God. We are called to operate as an effective team, in submission to one another, trusting that God will take care of our hearts as we do so.

The challenge here, again, is that shame brings condemnation, which causes us to isolate ourselves not only from God but from others around us. Submission to God and obeying His will through His word will open our hearts to act out in love, imitating our Creator.

Through the strength we gain by increasing our faith in what His plan is for our life, we will be able to exercise the same grace and forgiveness He has shown to others.

DEVELOPMENTAL KEY 6: Forgiveness

Forgiveness, key number six, is critical for our destiny to be realized. The Bible says if you do not forgive you shall not be forgiven (Luke 6:37). This tells me God is very serious about this point. Sometimes we may even find ourselves in situations in which we have to forgive somebody for situations that required police intervention. Clearly, I am not saying you must condone mistreatment of yourself or others, but forgiveness, even in serious situations is a necessity, even if we are the ones calling the police.

Forgiveness is critical, because when you are working on a team, people will offend you. If you are not slow to anger and quick to forgive, this will become detrimental to the advancement toward your destiny. If you have been offended, that means you are on the defense, and if you are on the defense, you are not moving forward. Therefore, be quick to forgive. God is love and His will is to provide grace and forgiveness. He wants us to imitate Him in this. Though this will not always be an easy thing, it is still necessary.

Jesus shows us a perfect model of submission to each other at the Last Supper when He washed the disciples' feet (John 13). Let's stop here for a second and think about this. Jesus, the Creator of everything that ever was and will be, humbled Himself by wrapping a towel around His waist, kneeling down, and washing the disciples' feet. What I find particularly amazing is He washed all of the disciples' feet, not just the ones that were loyal to Him. He also washed the feet of Judas, knowing full well he was about to deliver Him to the high priest and His eventual crucifixion on the cross. Now that is grace, forgiveness, and love!

The keys of submission, unity, faith, and trust are essential because of the treacherous nature of our journey and the war that constantly rages with the enemy. We have a mountain to take, and this can only be accomplished by yielding to the direction of the Holy Spirit in faith and in unity with the entire team, trusting that God is working out His plan.

Like summiting Everest, the guide works with individual members and the team as a whole to ensure its success. More critically, through the guide's great wisdom and experience, he will lead the team safely to the checkpoint camps along the way where the adequate sustenance and supplies await. These important camps are not just milestones in the climb to the summit, but they are required destination points each climber and team has to achieve to go on to the next heights.

This is also true on the journey to our destiny. There are certain points we must hit to continue to become stronger and to go higher. There are no shortcuts in climbing Everest, and so too, is this true in your life summit—your destiny. We cannot do this without the participation of the entire team working together or without complete trust in the guidance of the Holy Spirit and thus submitting to His authority. Expert guidance is essential in leading the team through the life threatening terrain, making sure they reach each camp on time and alive. Failure to submit to the wisdom of your guide or to work together as a team is likely to see your journey end prematurely or with catastrophic results. We can see over and over in scripture where obedience, or the lack there of, greatly changed the trajectory of one's life or even that of an entire nation—or greater still—the entire human race.

So if trust, submission, and obedience are so critical, why are they so hard to do? Why does it seem so elusive? Let's retrace ours steps back to the garden. We know the failure to submit causes disobedience, and this is what brought in the curse and sin nature. So if we have a sin nature, rebellion is more natural, and therefore is easier than obedience. The reason sin is so attractive is it feels good to our flesh. If sin did not feel good, why would you do it? This is why it is harder to obey than it is to disobey. It's like working out. We know what's good for us and we should do it. But again, it is harder to do what's good for us than it is to sit on the couch and each chips. However, this is where we need to re-evaluate.

Initially, though rebellion and disobedience may seem like the easier choice, like not working out and eating junk food for extended periods of time, they will exact increasingly high tolls from your life. The failure to submit and obey allows the curse that spans the generations to continue to cause you to live in fear, shame, and condemnation. This provides a perfect playground for the enemy to kill, steal, and destroy your life. But it will not end there. It creates a vicious cycle that many people live through time and time again, often passing it down to their children. Frequently it requires an outside person to intervene in order to break it. This curse that spans the generations is called a *generational curse.*

In chapter eight, "Breaking Past the Barriers," you will see I came from a very onerous background. If I were to go further back in my family lineage, you would see the same pattern playing out over and over again: failure to submit, disobedience, the entrance of the curse, fear expressed in anger and anxiety … Around and around it went, over the generations, and in my case, it took the power of God in Jesus Christ to set me free. Once set free, it required a process, the process of development, to help me deal with the issues generated by my family's generational curse. It also left me in a place where I had to make the right choices to bring about change in my life, and that of my children's lives, and therefore, change in my family lineage. Throughout this process I had to forgive; in some cases several times, to be free from my past. God is faithful, and He promises that who the Son sets free is free indeed (John 8:36). We just need to walk it out. I will deal with some of the roots of these issues and how we can work through them in greater detail in the next chapter.

If you are personally stuck in a cycle such as this one, do not worry. You are not alone, and there is hope for you as there was for me, in Jesus. The Bible has many situations in which people were stuck in such a cycle. One example is the children of Israel. God had delivered them from Egypt with many mighty signs, wonders, and miracles. They saw the nation of Egypt brought to its knees through plagues and eventually the killing of every firstborn son in the country. This led to Pharaoh finally letting the Israelite people go. Once they were free, God delivered them once again by the miraculous parting of the waters in the Red Sea, the act which also brought death to the entire Egyptian army that pursued them (Exodus 14). This removed the final obstacle and should have allowed them to move into the Promised Land. The Lord commanded them to go forward and possess it.

After all they have just come through, this should be a no-brainer, right? Sadly enough, this is not the case when fear is involved, as it produces anxiety and disobedience. This stage of their journey should have only taken days by foot. Unfortunately, after hearing the report from the twelve spies, they did not do as God instructed them. Fear gripped their hearts and prevented them from taking the next step in their destiny. As a result, they roamed as nomads around the same mountain for forty years.

This one act of disobedience caused the nation to lose an entire generation of people. All of the children of Israel, with the exception of Joshua and Caleb, outright denied the request God made for them to go and possess the Promised Land, because of the fear of the unknown. They saw the people in the land as giants and themselves as grasshoppers (Numbers 13:33), whereas God saw the Israelites as the giants and the people of the land as grasshoppers. Fear always gives you the wrong perspective and usually will compel you to act in disobedience. Faith, on the other hand, will compel you to obey God and do what He is calling you to do. Faith will give you the strength to move mountains rather than circle them. This is why God has given you His GPS in the Holy Spirit. It is not His desire to delay or in any way diminish your development process. On the contrary, His goal is to give you the fastest and most effective route.

But do not be discouraged! It is possible to be obedient (Developmental Key 1) to what God asks of us! There are people in the Bible we can learn from on the other side of the equation, the side of trust, faith, submission, and obedience. We can see how God was able to move in mighty ways because people were obedient and made the right decision. The right decision is almost always the hard one. Many times it can even seem crazy.

We see this in the story of Naaman (2 Kings 5). He was suffering from an incurable disease and therefore was extremely desperate, so desperate he traveled a long way to seek the prophet of God. The prophet told him to go and dip himself in the Jordan River seven times, and he would be healed from leprosy. I am sure this sounded as crazy then as it does now. I can testify that when you are desperate, you are willing to do some crazy things! At first he was angry at the simplicity of the prophet's instructions, but listening to those closest to him, he submitted.

I can just picture it in my mind. He is standing on the riverbank with those under his command all around, watching him, and thinking he has lost his mind. And there he is, dressed in his fancy clothes, walking into the river and going for it—going for his miracle! After the seventh dip, he became completely restored. It seems simple enough: go and get in the river then get healed. However, you have to look at the deeper context of the story to fully appreciate its significance. Naaman was a proud man and a great commander of an army. For him to humble himself in front of others, get down low and immerse himself in the dirty water was a truly significant act of obedience.

Another incredible event in the Bible in which one places obedience over understanding is in 1 Kings 17. Elijah meets a widow at the gates of a village. He tells her to make a cake out of the last bit of flour and oil she has left in the world and give it to him to eat. She obeys, and through her obedience, the Lord released a blessing that not only supplied food for Elijah, but for her and her son during a time of famine in the land.

Let's just stop for a minute and reconstruct this event. Imagine you were the widow. You have no spouse to help support you, and you have a child to care for. Food is more than scarce. You're about to prepare the only meal you will have before you starve and die, and a man you have never met comes up to you and tells you to give it to him instead. I believe if she did not obey, she would have died. However, through her obedience, God was able to deliver her from her current hopeless circumstances. Our God is a way-maker. He is able to make something from nothing. All He needs us to do is trust and obey, even when it seems crazy.

Many times when the Lord asks us to obey it can seem unusual, even counterintuitive. I have seen this to be very true in my own life. At the two-year mark in our business, we were prospering, and the Lord told me to move to a city over two hours away. We had no reason to move there other than a connection with some family members. Everything we had built and everything we had was in the city in which we were presently living. For us to relocate at that time seemed crazy, not only to me, but to everybody else around me. The incredulous question became: "You're going to keep the head office of your company in this city and move to another one over two hours away and run your business remotely?" I'm sure many people thought we were destined to fail.

As I write this book today, our business is in its tenth year, and rather than failing, it has become even more successful. That is not the biggest blessing, though. The biggest blessing is that the Lord led us to an amazing church with incredible people who have strengthened my marriage, my family, and my relationship with Him. The move helped me re-center my focus and realign my priorities. Interestingly enough, God's Positioning System leads us to where we *need* to go, not necessarily where we request to go! Sometimes God has to get you out of your current situation or circumstance to a place where He can speak to you. I can't say for certain, but I'm not sure this book would even exist if I hadn't obeyed the call of God and made that crazy leap to where He had called me.

This episode in my life reminds me of the story of Abraham. God spoke to him, calling him out from his home to move to a land far away where he did not know anybody and he had nothing. He did this on a promise—a promise that God would make his descendants as numerous as the grains of sand or stars in the sky (Genesis 15). With the single promise, Abraham put his faith and trust in the Lord and moved. This is why he is the father of faith.

By removing us from our comfort zone, God is able to bring us to a place where we must rely on Him alone and fully trust in Him. This situation is very uncomfortable, and this often makes people shrink back and not obey His call. If God has put you in this position, remember, it takes a leap of faith, but a leap for which He will prepare you. You can place your trust in Him and have faith in His plan and know that listening to His Holy Spirit will get you there.

Keep in mind, however, the Holy Spirit will get you where *you* need to go, not where someone else needs to go. An important aspect to understand in the area of obedience is its definitive nature. Being obedient to what you are *specifically* called to do is critical. As mentioned in chapter three, "Destiny Is a Team Sport," we are all part of the same body, but we all have our individual roles to play that are unique and specific to us—roles for which we have been explicitly prepared. It is important that as we are stepping out into what God is calling us to do, we are certain it is what we, as an individual, have been called to do within His plan. Being obedient is not trying to emulate anyone else or doing what they are called to do.

I have seen people try to emulate others people's teaching and speaking styles, or even step out and give away their entire paycheck because they heard an awesome testimony of how God blessed someone else who did this very thing. We have to understand those people were called to do that particular thing at that time to unlock that specific blessing God had prepared for them in advance. It is not necessarily for us. I'm not saying we don't learn from others. That can be just as important as well, but we must ensure *we* are doing what *we* are called to do.

At the same time, we must also be careful not to put our calling on other people. I have heard it said that *God wants to take care of the widows and orphans, and if everybody in the church is not doing so, they are not being the church.* I would say this, as well as many other things, is the Lord's heart, but it takes a large operation with many different inputs to see His will prevail. I may be called to be the part of the church that provides the human and financial resources to support an orphanage in another country. Just because I am not the boots on the ground does not mean I am not a part of what He wants to do in that area.

I think the misinterpretation of this belief has created many doctrinal issues, which has divided the church. We are all called to play our individuals parts to see the entire Kingdom of God prevail and advance. This could be on an individual, church, or even denominational level. The bottom line is we must all push forward together in unity for this common cause, each allowing our unique gifts and talents to advance the Kingdom.

Paul expresses this idea as he compares how God has given us each different spiritual gifts and abilities, but we need to all work together as one, just as all the parts of our physical bodies are different and equally valued, but together make up one body that functions as a unit (1 Corinthians 12:12–26).

Since everyone is given a unique path to follow and specific acts to obey, it is imperative you ensure that what you are obeying is from the Lord. There are several ways we can do this. First and foremost, make certain it lines up with Scripture. God will never stray from His Word. We can also talk to a trusted spiritual leader to make sure our personal perspective and our wounds do not cloud our judgment. And we, of course, can pray to clarify with the Lord that what we believe is actually what He wants us to do.

There may be times in our lives when we want to obey, but we feel like maybe we missed something along the way. Or, perhaps we simply did not obey the Lord. There is a parable in Matthew 21 that shows the way to redemption. It speaks of two sons. The father asks the older boy to go out and work in the vineyard. The son says, "No," but later changed his mind and went to work in the field. The second son said, "Yes sir, I will," but he didn't go. The parable is clear that the son who changed his mind and eventually obeyed, did the will of God. The fabulous thing about God's Positioning System is its brilliance in finding alternate routes that will connect back onto the path of destiny. All you need to do is follow the given directions.

So if you feel you have missed it or you have not obeyed God, you can simply change your mind and make a different choice right now. Turn back to Him. He is waiting and will open up an alternative route—a detour that will lead you back to the path of your destiny. We never go backward on our journey. Our God is in perpetual motion, and His river is flowing in one direction—onward and upward—toward your destiny. The transition back to the right path will always be gradual. A train cannot jump from one track to another quickly. If it tried to do so, it is easy to see it would be a disaster in the making. The decision to make the switch can happen quickly, but the process of working it out will take time. The transition will also take work, and it may even be painful, but you will be grafted back into your destiny, even further ahead than you were last time, as long as you have connected deeply enough to learn the lessons along the way.

God is a good Father and it pained Him to watch you make those decisions and go through those trials and tribulations. His plans are always to prosper you and bless you. He's our champion, friend, and Master Developer in the development process. Still today, He is causing all things to work together for good, as He did in the past. After the children of Israel had left Egypt, they made a bad decision, which resulted in them having to go around and around the mountain for forty years, but the victory was given when they made the right decision—the decision to embrace their destiny. From there, they took the land quickly. Could they have done it before? Were their wanderings actually necessary? I don't know what it would have looked like if they had made the right choice in the first place. The Bible does not address this point because it did not matter, simply because it did not happen.

Notice the Bible is not a book of alternate endings. God would not do this to us—having one decision you make lead to this destiny, and another leading to that one. There are many books and movies written about alternate endings; cue the movies *Back to the Future: Parts One, Two, and Three.* The enemy wants you to live in alternate endings: "I wish I would have done this," or "What would have happened if I had married this person?" This is especially true when trauma or loss are involved. The enemy will try to get you to spend years beating yourself up, hoping, and living in a false dream world. This is an extremely powerful temptation because in our regrets, we can create the perfect ending for our lives with all the perfect outcomes. The truth is, we are not perfect and we do not live perfect lives. That is why it is by the grace of God that He causes all things to work together for good. He weaves all our decisions, trials, and tribulations into the grand vision for our lives!

Therefore, do not worry! You are not behind on your path, and you did not waste too much time, causing your destiny to suffer for it. No matter where you are in your journey or where you think you should be along the path—even if you fear you've failed or taken a wrong turn or two—you only need to consult God's GPS to get back to exactly where you need to be. He, the Lord of all creation, will fulfill your destiny in your life, one way or another, with you as His partner! Your role is simply to seek Him with all your heart and begin to understand the truth of how God sees you and who you are in Christ.

CHAPTER 7

The Penguin King

AT NIGHT BEFORE MY KIDS GO TO SLEEP, I ENJOY TAKING TIME out to tell them stories. Since I cannot read to them from a book, I have to create the stories as I tell them. This leaves me trusting God for the storylines, and He tends to lead us on many strange and wonderful adventures. Sometimes my kids become cowboys, transported to the Wild West, facing down dastardly outlaws. Other times they are kings and queens with amazing powers to rule realms with great authority and wisdom, receiving divine guidance from something that cannot be seen.

One particular night I was telling my children a story about two heroines who were traversing through a very cold, difficult tundra wasteland. The journey had taken them to a huge mountain they had to overcome. While climbing, they were captured by some penguins. These penguins brought them into the middle of the mountain and through a secret door hidden in the rock face, where there was a large ice cavern. Here was found a throne room, and in the throne room was the penguin king. He was a proud king with a big crown and he had many subjects who bowed down to him. The penguin king LOVED when his subjects bowed down to him.

The other thing the king loved was riddles. He believed himself to be the wisest of the penguins, and he had a riddle nobody had ever been able to solve, though they had tried for many, many years. The king decided to make a wager with the captured young heroines. "If you can solve my riddle, I will let you go," he challenged them. "If you cannot, you will become my slaves and have to bow down to me."

The young heroines, not seeing any other option, decided to take him up on his proposition. The penguin king arrogantly recited the riddle: "You can't see me, but you can see the effects of my presence. You can feel me all around you and sometimes you can even hear me, but you cannot touch me. What am I?"

After much pondering and discussion, our clever, young heroines were able to solve his riddle and their dilemma. With authority, they provided the answer in unison. The answer was, "You are the wind!" The penguin king let out a yell in his defeat, "NOOOO!" Our two heroines had to be set free!

This is how many of us feel about God. He can seem like a mystery or a riddle we need to decipher, which poses a significant challenge if the Holy Spirit is supposed to be your guide to the plan the Father has for your life. So then, why does God seem so intangible and difficult to connect with? We can hear Him now and again in the words that are whispered into our ears by the Holy Spirit. Other times something connects with our spirit when we are reading the Bible, resonating deep within us. Or maybe a message is delivered directly to our hearts by the prophetic words of someone else. We can even feel Him if we are fortunate enough to find ourselves in His presence, shouldering the weight of His glory. We can see the effects of Him all around us in creation, but we cannot see Him in a physical form, let alone do we feel like we can touch Him.

Sometimes our destiny seems to share this same slight elusiveness. We have heard it spoken to us. We can feel it drawing us—even propelling us forward—begging us to pursue it. More astounding is that as we are given glimpses of our destiny from time to time, it often seems so fantastic, so large, so enormous, we think it could not possibly be true. We do not believe enough in ourselves to fathom that we would be able to do such amazing things. The real truth though, is we serve an amazing God who delights in us and loves giving us great gifts, including an amazing purpose for our lives. The truth of those glimpses, or sneak peaks He gives us, is found in the fulfillment of our life's calling in His Son, Jesus. He has created us for these amazing things to fulfill His purpose on the earth. However, we do need to go through the process of development to get there.

Overcoming Fear, Rejection, and False Beliefs

This inability to connect with the larger vision for our lives—our destiny—stems from the shame and condemnation that comes from sin, as previously outlined. The shame separates us from God and the relationship He wants to have with us. As explained in Genesis 3, after Adam and Eve partook of the fruit and sin entered in, their next step was to cover themselves with fig leaves in shame and hide from the Father. This separation from our heavenly Father and His love and protection opens the door for fear to enter our lives. This poses a significant problem for us because fear is simply the absence of faith.

We have already learned that faith is foundational in engaging with the will of God for our lives, and exercising this faith strengthens us so we can carry the weight of our destiny. This is because it gives us the understanding we need to trust Him in order for our destiny to be fulfilled. So if we are under shame and condemnation, thus allowing fear to come in, we are opening ourselves up to the enemy and to the lies which he is ever so eager to speak into our minds. These lies are often sown during an event of trauma in our lives, and they can take root at a very early age. If the devil can infiltrate your mind with these lies early enough and they are not broken, it gives him extraordinary power over your future.

We see this in Genesis 3:7–11 when the Father came to Adam and Eve and saw them covered in fig leaves. He asked them where they were. After Adam had confessed he was hiding because he was naked, God asked him who had told him he was naked, knowing full well what had happened. This makes it very clear that the enemy had spoken this lie into their lives. These lies that are spoken into our lives and then held as truths form something called a **false belief system**. False beliefs we have about ourselves cause us to react to many situations and scenarios in an adverse manner. The enemy will use these false beliefs to control you and stop you from moving forward until these lies are exposed and broken.

Through my experience in counseling, both in training and in working with people, I strongly believe the root of most of the fear we have stems from rejection or the fear of it. This leads to insecurities within us that mask themselves in many different ways so as not to be exposed. I believe this rejection, or the fear of it, is one of the primary causes of the issues we face in our lives. Though I do not discount other sources, such as genetic disposition, for the purpose of this book and helping us to understand the development process, I'm focusing on the aspect that directly impacts us in the pursuit of our destiny.

At first glance, having one root as the fundamental cause for the majority of our issues may seem unrealistic. But as you stop to reflect on your own life's situations and scenarios, understanding will grow. Let's delve a little more into the concept of rejection and the fear of it, so that we can understand this at a deeper level.

As we reflect on that garden scene immediately after the fall of man, God, in concert with Himself, decided He had to drive man out of the garden so they would not partake of the tree of life and live forever in a fallen state. This is the first incident of rejection recorded in history.

What is interesting to me is that this was done to protect us not to harm us. This was done out of love and not out of evil. The devil, however, perverts everything. He uses the false belief system and the separation brought on from shame to lie to us. I can imagine him whispering into Adam and Eve's ears, "God doesn't love you or He would never have done this to you." When we listen to these lies of the enemy and yield to the false belief system, we often subject ourselves to self-rejection.

Believing a lie based on what other people think about us, even if they have not vocalized it, is another trap of rejection that forms a virtual prison in our mind. This prison can be painful and cause us to do almost anything to prevent the pain of rejection from returning. Often, fear of this very pain is what compels us. Fear can be very broad and sometimes very unassuming. You could have a fear of failure because if you fail someone, they will reject you, which could cause you to have a people-pleasing or performance oriented mentality. Or, on the other side of the spectrum is the fear of what might happen if you do succeed. This does not necessarily mean the fear of success itself, but rather the fear of not knowing what happens after achieving the success. This uncertainty can lead you to self-sabotage and to just outright freeze to prevent yourself from succeeding at a task or job.

The first level in understanding how this plays out is to realize rejection expresses itself in many ways in your life, stemming from the false belief systems. Common false belief systems sound like, "I will never be good enough to succeed, so why should I even bother trying?" Or, "If they find out who I really am, they won't accept me." This often results in the creation of a mask of perfection. These beliefs usually stem from early traumatic incidents in our lives where the enemy was able to insert a lie. The lie provided the foundation for him to build on so he could try to take control of us. This lie, planted so early in our lives at a time of trauma and vulnerability, acts as a seed that grows and produces the false belief system.

The Bible says, "As a man thinks in his heart, so is he" (Proverbs 23:7 NKJV). That being the case, if the enemy can get you to believe things about yourself that are not true, it is easier to trigger you to respond from that position, rather than from the truth of who you really are as a child of the King. These false belief systems lead to coping behaviors such as drinking too much wine, excessive spending, comfort eating, being a workaholic and so on, to cover up the hurt.

The list of ways rejection can present itself, and the false belief systems that result in coping mechanisms are extensive and far beyond the scope of this book. But let's look at some of the most common situations so you can examine your own life and recognize this root. In this way, you can be freed, empowering you to pursue your destiny unencumbered. As you take the time at the end of the chapter to reflect on your life and analyze it, I am certain you will be able to trace each issue back to a lie the enemy was able to sow into your life, resulting in some form of rejection, usually at the time of a traumatic incident.

Once you have identified the entrance point of the lie and the resulting rejection in your life, you can ask God to set you free from it and help you to forgive those who hurt you. Then, with the power of the Holy Spirit, you can begin to heal the trauma resulting from believing the lie.

This healing is critical because rejection and the fear of it lead us to react irrationally to a whole host of situations. The fear can be so paralyzing it can actually stop us from engaging with our destiny. There may be situations in your life when you just wanted to run away rather than face it or deal with it. Or the opposite can happen: you suddenly fly across the room in a fit of anger and rage, triggered by some inconsequential matter, without even understanding fully why you reacted so violently. Depression, anxiety, self-hatred, and many other inward or outward expressions can all stem from rejection. These early traumatic events create the filter through which we perceive our environment and react to the world around us.

Since the fall of Adam and Eve, all of humanity comes into this world as a negative because of the resulting sin nature. I have children, and one thing I did not have to teach them was to lie or to be mean. It came naturally. That is not to say all kids are mean little liars. Having four of them myself, I would tell you they are my perfect little angels. We have to remember though, like us, they too were brought into this world as a negative with sin nature. This is why our entire life is a process—a journey of developing that negative into the picture the Father saw at the beginning. It is because of sin nature, and the fact the enemy comes to kill, steal, and destroy (John 10:10), that people naturally hurt other people, causing rejection wounds.

You can see this in Genesis 3 with Adam and Eve. Since the Bible doesn't specifically talk about Adam and Eve's parenting skills, one can only imagine. They were the first parents ever, and they were now dealing with their own failure and rejection issues. I believe, like all of us, they were not perfect parents. They gave birth to the first two of their children, Cain and Abel. These were the first children born into sin nature; the first ones that were actually brought into the world as negatives.

This leads to the second story of rejection in the Bible, in Genesis 4, when Cain killed his brother, Abel. I can only imagine the pain it caused in the first family. Why did he kill his brother? Because of rejection. This is where the cycle of rejection continued.

I have learned that hurt people hurt other people. The Lord rejected Cain's offering. This was too much for him to bear. He was hurt and in turn, he hurt his brother to the ultimate degree—he killed him. However, it is important to understand God did not reject Cain as a person. Abel's animal sacrifice covered his sin in the blood of the lamb he gave, whereas Cain's offering of grain did not. God could not forgive the sin nature unless the sacrifice was given with coverage in the blood. Genesis 4 continues the account as Cain was driven away from his family. He settled in another land and built a city. Cain went on to multiply and raise up a whole race of hurt people. Not long after this, you see wars beginning to break out. Again, the basic principle is that hurt people hurt people.

This whole concept of rejection and the resulting fear ties in to our pursuit of destiny because it is one of the biggest weapons the enemy uses against us to try to stop us from fulfilling it. He uses this strategy to attack us at a very young age in an attempt to prevent us from rising up into the full truth of what the Lord has for our lives. This very thing has happened throughout our history. We can read in the Bible where the enemy used King Herod to try to kill Jesus when He was first born (Matthew 2:13). In Exodus 1, King Pharaoh ordered the death of all the newborn Hebrew males as the enemy tried to kill

Moses, whose destiny was to become the great emancipator for the Israelite people.

Just as the Lord works through people, so does the enemy of our destiny. He will use this rejection cycle and those people in our lives who are closest to us in an attempt to scare us, anger us, and stop us from being able to move forward in our destiny. The bigger truth, however, the more powerful one, is that our God is a healer and we can be completely free from the wounds of this destructive cycle. The first step is to fully understand how this whole cycle works and its effects on us as negatives.

The Limbic System

The rejection cycle begins when we are young, and we start to incur trauma. This trauma becomes an integral part of our internal programming. The memories of these events are engraved onto a part of our brain called the limbic system. It is from this limbic system that our reactions to various situations, dramatic or otherwise, originate.

Please note we are referring to our 'reactions,' not actions. Reactions are usually impulsive and come as a result of a trigger being pressed, while actions are thought out and planned. There is a significant difference between these two. There are three limbic responses: fight, flight, and freeze. These responses were engraved in our brains very early in our lives to protect us from natural situations that could threaten our very life.

In the beginning, these instincts kept us alive. If you see a lion or another animal with big teeth wanting to make you his lunch, your limbic system engages, telling you there is danger, and you run. Or perhaps you return home from work, and you see an enemy attacking your home, harming the ones you love. Anger rises up, the limbic system engages again, and you fight.

However, the response of freezing, interestingly enough, only seems to have a detrimental effect. For example, a threatening situation occurs, and the limbic system response is to absolutely freeze—to not move or do anything at all. There are many recorded instances where people have frozen in life or death situations and consequently died. More commonly, we see this in situations in which people are scared of the potential outcome, or they feel incapable, so they freeze by procrastinating their engagement with the event. In essence, they do nothing. They will continue to put everyone and everything off, time and time again, even if this reaction has dire consequences.

Though the freeze response is clearly adverse, the fight and flight responses can also be destructive. As noted earlier, flying off the handle in an uncontrolled outburst can result in abusive situations with the people we love becoming the focus of our rage. This reaction causes us to do things we would not normally otherwise do, such as hurt those who are closest to us. This type of reaction obviously has significant short- and long-term consequences, such as the story of Cain and Abel.

In regards to the destructive impact of the flight response, we don't have to look far to see the statistics. Over forty percent of homes in North America, primarily Canada and the United States, are fatherless. Men who are not able to rise up and deal with certain situations choose to run, and women are not immune to this choice either. Along with absolute flight, this response can also lead people to engage in conflict avoidance, keeping them from making necessary decisions, which can produce harmful consequences.

With all three limbic system responses causing possible negative repercussions, it is well worth exploring them a little further. If you search for the causes of these types of engravings on our limbic system, you will find there is no perfect answer because we are all unique people with endlessly different types of upbringings. Nevertheless, there are some common denominators for incurring the trauma that ultimately formats this system.

The first to consider are severe incidents such as car accidents, natural disasters, deaths, or abuse. These are hard not to overlook. However, trauma can hide in many forms and be much more subtle than we often expect. It will also look different for every person, which sometimes makes it difficult to spot. For some, it can be traumatizing to fail at something that they've worked hard at to succeed. Or, they could have been embarrassed by a parent, a teacher, or even by their peers in the middle of a classroom. There is such a large variety of seemingly minor incidents that can cause trauma that Holy Spirit discernment can be necessary to track it down.

Healing the Cycle

Once you take a moment to reflect back on your life with the help of the Holy Spirit, I'm sure there will be situations that will come to your mind that will make you feel a pang in your stomach. For me, that gut check is usually linked with a specific traumatic situation in my life. This situation is what's called a trigger or a button. When something or someone hits this trigger, it causes one of the reactions (usually an overreaction) of flight, fight, or freeze from the limbic system to engage, and we react, sometimes illogically, rather than responding rationally to the situation.

The key is to identify these triggers so the wounds that caused them can be healed. Once a wound is healed, the trigger in that area is removed, so you will no longer overreact. Some wounds will necessitate deeper healing and may require you to meet with someone, perhaps even an expert or professional, to get complete resolution and healing. The Holy Spirit, however, is there and available to help you through this healing process.

Though the complete healing process cannot be fully encompassed in this book, there are a few things you can do to begin reprogramming your limbic system. First, when a trigger is hit, take a moment to pray. Ask God to take you to the memory of the incident that caused this wound. Then ask the Holy Spirit to help you forgive those involved and to heal the wound. Secondly, when thoughts come into your mind that are not in alignment with the Word or what God's will is for your life, simply refuse to partner with them. Declare out loud that you will not do so! Thirdly, begin to think on what is true, honorable, right, and pure. Think about things that are excellent and worthy of praise (Phil 4:8). Remember, this is a process and will take time, but it will enable you to reprogram your limbic system. You will be able to act rather than react. The impact of this change in your life for you and those around you will be immeasurable.

Since forgiveness is a key in the healing cycle as well as in our destiny, let's explore it a little further. Like most things in the Kingdom, healing begins with forgiveness. To reiterate, please note this does not mean you have to condone what they did, nor do you have to trust them again, but you do need to forgive them in order to begin your own healing.

Unforgiveness is much like a tug-of-war. You are on one end of the rope and whoever harmed you is on the other end. You can battle them as long as you want. Sometimes these people are even dead. Some people engage in the tug-of-war battle in their sleep, all night long, and they wake up exhausted. What would happen if you let go of the rope? I will tell you. The war is over. It does not matter what the other person on the other end of the rope does, because as soon as you let go, you are free! Again, you may have to go through the process of forgiving many times over, but you will be freed from it as long as you persevere.

Unfortunately, this does not necessarily mean your limbic system will be instantly changed. When the limbic system engages, your brain releases a whole host of chemicals your body feels it needs. But, your brain can actually be reprogrammed over time. Healing is the beginning of this and then walking out your healing is the next step. This process will take some time, but if you put your trust in the Holy Spirit and yield yourself to the development process, God the Father will help you with this. This is a powerful truth of the development process. It is there to set you free from the curse brought on mankind through the fall of Adam and Eve. Through the process of developing the negative, we will become free from the things that ensnare us.

Now let's return once again to our penguins. It wasn't until writing this chapter and reflecting on the story the Lord gave me that I came to realize some of the symbolism. You, like the two heroines, are the hero of your journey, traveling through the development process. The penguins symbolize the enemy, and the mountain symbolizes the past hurts and trials we need to get over in order to continue to press through to the fulfillment of our destiny. Just like in the story, the enemy wants to take you and place you under the mountain (your past hurts) and put you in service to the penguin king, who is the enemy of our destiny.

It is vital you fully grasp the understanding that everything the devil does stems from a seed of a lie. As long as you are encased in your past hurts and trials, you cannot be progressing on your journey toward the fulfillment of your destiny. However, just like in the story, God is the answer. And everything God does and is, stems from the seed of truth. But unlike the wind, we can reach out and touch Him. Just like a woman with the issue of blood touched Him and was completely healed and set free, if you reach out and touch Him, power will come from Him, and you will be healed and restored (Mark 5:25–34). So whatever your past, whatever your hurts, push through, push hard, and reach for your destiny!

Now it's your turn. Take this time to reflect back on your life to begin your road to healing. Think about the things in your life you believe may be expressions of rejection. Take a moment and pray. Ask the Holy Spirit to show you the specific incidents where rejection has entered your life. As He reveals the entrance points, ask Jesus to heal the memory. Ask Him to show you how He helped you through it. Then take the courageous step of forgiving those who hurt you so your healing can begin. Let go of that tug-of-war rope!

NOTE: This chapter has touched on concepts found in the Genesis process. If you'd like to learn more about it please visit *www.genesisprocess.org*.[7]

CHAPTER 8

Breaking Past the Barriers

BARRIERS ARE DESIGNED TO STOP MOVEMENT—EITHER KEEPING something in or preventing something from getting out. This can be beneficial in our natural world, but when these barriers seep into the mental and emotional realm of our hearts and minds, they become limiting forces that can trap us in negative mindsets. They keep us from moving forward in our lives.

Many situations can lead us to build walls. Experiences of rejection have the detrimental by-product of erecting such barriers that can prevent us from even starting our journey in the process of development. We will often disqualify ourselves, counting ourselves out, for seemingly good reasons. In the natural realm, these reasons may seem perfectly rational. One such reason could be a physical limitation. As you now know, this is one I have struggled with personally. It has impacted me greatly over the course of my life, even before I was physically limited.

When I was twenty-five years old, I was invited to a Jewish hot tub party, and that is where I met my future wife. Okay, it really wasn't a Jewish hot tub party. There weren't actually people wandering around in Jewish attire reading the Torah or anything. Okay, there weren't even any Jewish people there at all. A friend who was house sitting for some Jewish people invited me to a hot tub party she was having. That is where I met my wife, the most wonderful woman in the world.

I was drawn to her instantly, and I knew I liked her. She, however, took things a lot slower. She is definitely a processor. At first, we ended up being good friends for several months. We would talk for hours and hours and ended up building a strong relationship. The truth is, she was much too good for me, and it took that long of dogged persistence to convince her to give me a shot!

The only problem was I was hiding a secret—the secret that I was losing my eyesight and was eventually going to go blind. As the relationship moved along and became more serious, I grew fearful she would reject me. So instead of waiting for that to happen, I started to reject her first. I began to self-sabotage by repeatedly breaking up with her in hopes of keeping her from finding out I was going to go blind and then rejecting me because of it.

I still clearly remember the day my theory was put to the test. We were driving to her parents' house. They lived in a small town two hours away from where we were both living at the time (separately of course). The scenery was monotonous. The land was very flat, and the crops were blowing back-and-forth in the wind. For the sake of context, my vision was still pretty good at this point. As we were driving in what for me was silent boredom, she turned to me, and she said, "I know what's going to happen to you."

I responded, "What do you mean?"

"With your eyes," she replied. "I researched it. You're going to go blind," she said. I thought this was it; this was the time I had been dreading. She was going to tell me she could no longer see me. In my mind, I counted myself out even before she finished the sentence. However, that is not at all what she said. Instead of rejecting me because of my eventual physical limitation, she accepted me. She showed me Christ-like love. I was shocked. I didn't even know how to deal with it then, and to this day, I'm still amazed by the turn of events. But, I do understand it to be a powerful symbol of the grace of God.

You may not have eyesight issues, but maybe you think you are too old or have committed some sin from which you cannot be redeemed. Perhaps you struggle with other health issues, impairments, or mobility challenges. It may even be problems in the area of mental health or that you have suffered great emotional trauma from which you are still recovering. There are an endless number of things that can cause us to disqualify ourselves from staying the course God has chosen for us.

The enemy wants you to shrink back, even right down to depression if he can get you that far, forcing you to believe you are broken and not worthy. Or he will try to get you to think maybe God is angry with you. He will whisper in your ear, "If He wasn't angry with you, He would have healed you already. He is a loving God after all, isn't He?" This is a lie from the pit of hell. The truth is we are all healed in Christ, and we are just waiting for that healing to manifest. Manifestation may not come in the timing we want, but it will come.

This does not disqualify us nor should it prevent us from engaging in and moving along our journey of development. I have found that pushing through this particular barrier opens tremendous doors and can be very inspiring for those who are around us. We have to remember that our God is an eternal God, and He sees things from an eternal perspective—so different from our limited vision. This body we have is an earthly vessel that will pass away and cannot be brought with us to eternity.

Another common barrier we construct is financial limitation. It is very often the case that in the natural, we do not have the financial resources available to fund our destiny on our own. But this is exactly where the Lord wants us, and this is where He comes in. He will provide the *provision* where He provides the *vision*. This is a key to understanding, and it is a very good area in which to develop your faith. Fear often causes us to hold on to the little we may have, but as long as you are holding on to what is in your hand, it is impossible for you to grab hold of what God is giving you from His hand. This is why the Bible tells us to sow generously (2 Corinthians 9:6). God does not need our money; He needs our obedience. 1 Samuel 15:22 says obedience is better than sacrifice. We see this in the garden. If Adam and Eve had simply obeyed and not eaten the fruit, they would have avoided thousands of years of unnecessary animal sacrifices to reconcile with God. Once we obey the Word and follow Him, again, He can add His super to our natural. I had to learn this obedience in my life.

One morning, the Lord woke me up around 3:00 a.m. and began to speak to me about the principle of tithing. Chapter 23 in Matthew takes this decree to the heart: "What sorrow awaits you teachers of religious law and you Pharisees. Hypocrites! For you are careful to tithe even the tiniest income from your herb gardens, but you ignore the more important aspects of the law—justice, mercy, and faith. You should tithe, yes, but do not neglect the more important things. You are so careful to clean the outside of the cup and the dish, but inside you are filthy—full of greed and self-indulgence! You blind Pharisee! First wash the inside of the cup and the dish, and then the outside will become clean, too" (23, 25–26 NLT).

This rebuke from Jesus reflects their hypocritical nature of concerning themselves more about outward appearances than with the condition of their heart. In their hypocrisy, they were so conscious about the outward appearance of following the law in absolute precision that they even tithed on the smallest thing, practically right down to a mint leaf. Yet, the inside condition of their heart showed filth and greed.

This seems to frame people who tithe and the act itself in a very negative light. I instead, wanted to be a cheerful giver like the Bible says (2 Corinthians 9:7) and not a Pharisee who only tithes religiously. I wanted to be one that was moved by the Spirit and one who let the Lord lead my heart.

I didn't know why at the time, but I had always thought Jesus said we did not have to tithe, as this was Old Testament law. It was almost like I was blind to this fact of the Scriptures. I did give, and I gave more than ten percent, but I did not want to be tied to a religious law that would hold me back. The truth was, once I reflected on this, and the Lord took me to the Scriptures and showed me how tithing is actually a New Testament principle, I could reflect back in my life to a time when I was hurt by a spiritual leader. This hurt caused me to want to be in control of my finances and where they went rather than obeying the Scriptures. This was a perfect opportunity to practice forgiveness. I had to forgive the one who had hurt me and ask the Holy Spirit to heal that trust wound. Once that happened, I was free to move along in my process of development!

As soon as I was free from this wound, I became excited about tithing, and within twelve months I was able to give quadruple what I was giving the previous year. And it has been growing ever since. The amazing thing about this is that God has grown the pie for me and increased the amount that was coming in because of this obedience. Once again, this is what He needs—our obedience, not our money. Don't let financial lack be a barrier to fulfilling your destiny.

Another factor that creates barriers for many people is life circumstances. People get busy being busy. There are practical reasons for being busy: family, work, functions, and activities. There are also specific seasons we go through in which our priorities have to shift, and that is an important point to make. My wife is an amazing mother to our four children, and I know in the weeks following a birth, it would be impossible for her to go out and do anything that did not pertain to her healing or to the baby. This is both in a physical capacity, but also from a priority perspective. Going back to the aforementioned list of priorities, even though serving God is number one, He will not cause us to put our family on the altar and sacrifice them in the name of ministry or destiny. I have often found that these seasons are times of preparation and internal growth. Sometimes you don't even know you're growing. It is like the tree. The tree grows most in the winter. Though there's no outward expression of growth, such as leaves and fruit, it is expanding its capacity and deepening its roots. We therefore need to understand this principle, so we can maximize the growing seasons in our lives.

Work or school can also be an unconscious barrier, holding us back from pushing forward. We may feel we need to get a promotion, earn a degree or achieve some status. These things can be beneficial, and they may even be a critical part of our destiny, but they cannot be our sole focus. We must continue to push on and bloom wherever God plants us. We need to be aware of what's going on around us in all seasons. God often uses your current situation to develop you and further you along in your process. It is important to do the things that are right before you, and this will lead to the fulfillment of your calling.

Many people confuse seasons in their life with barriers. We all go through seasons as we grow. These seasons can be such things as parenthood, educational endeavors, or serving in a ministry. Whatever it is, seasons are used in our development process to prepare us for the fulfillment of our destiny. It is important to not mistakenly believe that because you are doing certain things in life, you cannot be moving along your path to destiny. We can compare it to Daniel in the movie *The Karate Kid*. Daniel was a young man who was being bullied at school by a guy who knew karate. In order to defend himself and stand up to the bully, Daniel sought out a karate sensei, Mr. Miyagi. Mr. Miyagi agreed to teach Daniel-san karate, and told him to come to his home to begin his training. Mr. Miyagi had Daniel doing many seemingly useless chores around his place, such as washing cars and painting fences. (I love the wax on, wax off scene!) By the second day of this seemingly useless training, Daniel was frustrated and wanted to quit. This is when Mr. Miyagi began to spar with Daniel-san, showing him the power of what he had just learned. The very things Daniel-san thought were meaningless were actually the things that were preparing him to fulfill his destiny as the Karate Kid. The lesson here is not to confuse seasons in your life with barriers. God will use all things to work together for good in the fulfillment of your destiny. So be intentional and continue to look for the God-given opportunities in everyday events.

DEVELOPMENTAL KEY 7: Identity in Christ

Another huge builder of barriers can be your personal history. This can include everything that has happened to you in the past and even where you come from, socio-economic status, race, and religion, to name only a few. I, if anyone, could be one of those people who could count myself out because of where I came from.

I grew up in an extremely poor family in the hood of my city. We were so poor it was not uncommon for us to dumpster dive behind our local 7-Eleven to search for food among what others would consider waste. As long as it wasn't moldy, you know, the green inspection, we would eat the food from the trash. The best days were when we would find old subs and sandwiches that we would salvage to feed our large family.

I still remember the feeling of the cold, hard dumpster as I put my hand up on the edge to pull myself over the top and land in its deep, smelly inside, almost as if I was swallowed whole. I was always scared the garbage truck would come and empty the bin while I was in it. The walls were covered with filth that had built up over the years. I always tried not to brush against it and get it on my clothes. The worst part was the wretched smell. At times it was too terrible to bear. But bear it I did. It was a necessary evil under the circumstances. We were in there not only to find old food, but bottles and cans as well. This is how our family survived.

My father was not a perfect man, but he always managed to put some type of food on the table, and he kept a roof over our heads. He had grown up in a very difficult training school where he was often abused. He only had a grade three education, which had been a significant limitation in his life, and why my father was a garbage man. We therefore had to pick bottles and cans from anywhere we could find them to pay the bills.

I remember one of the first times this happened. We rumbled to a stop at the 7-Eleven in my dad's blue truck with the large, homemade metal bumper grill. My dad jumped out and walked up to the garbage can. I had wondered what he was doing. Then I knew. He popped off the top of the can that stood in front of the store and began to rummage through the trash, right in front of everyone! He pulled out all the bottles and cans he could find. This was a real defining point in my life. This is where I understood the depths of our poverty. I had a sudden sinking feeling in my stomach. I slunk low in my seat, low enough that my head was below the truck's dash so nobody could see me in my shame. That was a stark realization. We were already eating Puffed Wheat with only water and using sugar and water for hairspray, but this was a whole new level of poverty to understand, even for my young brain. So I did what most young seven-year-old boys would do. I went to work to help the family.

After moving into a rental house in a new neighborhood, I remember biking up and down the alleys looking in the trash cans to see if I could find any treasures to take home. I was, after all, an entrepreneur even at this young age. At the end of one particular alley, I saw a large building. Large buildings were always good because that meant that they had large garbage bins with the possibility of large treasures. I pulled up to the building. It was a not-so-exclusive golf course. I decided to go in to ask for a job. Though this may seem like an insignificant part of the story, this was the choice, knowingly or not, that engaged me with my destiny. I was making the most of the season I was in, even at seven years old, and grabbing hold of the opportunities in front of me. This was my karate kid moment.

I walked up to the desk where a man named Steve, who turned out to be the club manager, was standing. He was wearing beige pants and a golf shirt that matched the color of the golf course. I asked him if there were any jobs I could do, like picking up golf balls or something, to earn some money. Steve gave me a big, warm smile. He said, "Yes." The job, in its essence was simple: take a large trash can—I don't know if you remember the metal ones we used to put in the back alley, exactly like the one Oscar the Grouch lived in on Sesame Street—and fill it with the muddy golf balls from the driving range that the tractor could not collect.

The golf course was nestled in a valley with residential houses on one side and apartments on the other. I imagine the city designer using the golf course to split the two types of residential dwellings apart from each other. The course had a large driving range with a total distance of about 500 yards. The driving range started at the top of the hill by the single dwelling homes, near the actual golf course itself, and descended all the way down to a mostly dirt bottom. At about 300 yards, there was a large pool of water about eighty feet in length and about fifteen to twenty feet wide, depending on the amount of rainfall that season. This mud hole collected a lot of golf balls from the clients of the driving range. The tractor that pulled a golf ball picker behind it worked well to collect most of the balls on the driving range, with the exception of the errant balls in the muddy pit.

I remember pulling the trash can down the hill thinking, *Man I'm going to be rich!* I then wondered, *Is this what rich people do? Hit balls into a big valley?* It didn't make much sense to me, as this was my very first exposure to the game of golf. I reached the mud hole and set my trash can on the edge of the mud. Now you have to remember, this was the eighties, and things were different back then. I was down there in the mud picking up golf balls, while people were hitting them over my head, with no thought of my safety at all.

The balls were whizzing by on my left and my right. I was like a duck on a firing range. This was hard work. As I continued to pick up the balls and place them in the trash can, I realized this was turning out to be more than I had bargained for. The ones on the edge were okay, but the ones closer to the middle were going to be more challenging. The deeper I trenched into the water, the deeper the mud, and the harder it was to lift my feet up from the bottom. I'm sure you have experienced this. *Splat!* Your foot goes into the mud. It sinks down and down, and the mud comes over the top of your foot, and all of a sudden, you are stuck! And so I was stuck.

I pulled and pulled on my leg, and I couldn't get my foot out! Then all of a sudden, pop! Out came my foot. The only problem was there was no shoe attached to it. Once I retrieved my shoe, I realized it would be easier to do this barefoot and away I went, shoeless, wading into the mud hole, and picking up the balls.

No one can ever really count the time in these types of situations.

For me, it was an eternity. It wasn't a funny point in my life. But after what seemed to be about a half-day's work, the bucket was finally full! I was very excited, but then I realized I wasn't done yet. I had to get this heavy bucket full of golf balls back up to the top of the hill. This was going to be no easy feat; I was a small seven-year-old boy and this bucket definitely weighed more than I did.

But I would not be denied. I began to pull, push, and drag that old trash can back up the hill. As I was doing this, more and more people began to gather around, and as they watched me, they started to cheer me on. This was powerful for me. When I finally got my prize possession, my bucket full of balls, to the top of the hill, Steve was standing there with a big smile on his face. He presented me with my very first crisp five-dollar bill. I still remember to this day, the picture on it and everything. There was no need to frame the money, nor the moment. They would be forever engrained in my memory.

With that single act, Steve had given me a gift that would forever change my life. The gift, or should I say key, was for me to realize it was possible for me to be someone more than a scrawny, dirty poor boy from the hood. I had the opportunity to be able to achieve a level of greatness. This is the seventh developmental key—know your identity in Christ. Know you are a child of the King, and with that inheritance, anything is possible!

Reflecting back on this now that I am much older and have children of my own, I know my Father was there, and He was cheering me on. The journey to our destiny is much like my journey of pulling that trash can to the top of the hill. It was hard, full of struggles, and sometimes I wanted to quit. But there was a crowd of great witnesses cheering me on to finish, and I was able to do just that. And that is what is happening in heaven right now. God the Father and the crowd of witnesses are cheering you on (Hebrews 12:1).

Though the victory over the trash can was a momentous occasion, it did not mean my life was great from that point on. On the contrary, in many ways it became more difficult. I do believe though, that we have these glimpses throughout our lives to encourage us and to spur us on into our destiny. Even though coming from a poor family and a poor neighborhood caused much difficulty in my life, even to this day, I still have a choice to make. Yes, there is a reality in the truth of where I came from, but I do not have to let it define who I am, nor where I am going. And neither do you. Do not let your past history, reality, or choices define who you are or who you will become. Break past the barriers and choose the destiny God has for you.

CHAPTER 9

The Pinocchio Trap

In today's society, the term *idol* can have many meanings and connotations, from an amazing singer and someone we look up to, to an object representing a deity that is worshiped and adored. In the world today there are millions and millions of people who bow down to actual statues and other images carved or fabricated in the image of what they believe is a deity. These traditional idols, such as handcrafted statues of Buddha and the like, require the offering of sacrifices and the burning of incense in order to worship them. Christians recognize these as false gods, and would not unknowingly worship any of them. However, in our western culture, the idolatry we practice has taken on a more subtle form, but it is just as treacherous and even more deceptive. And these idols, the ones we hold nearest and dearest to our hearts, are the ones that are culturally accepted. We have ended up putting much costlier things on the altar of worship to our idols than a plaster statue.

In the Old Testament, we can see the children of Israel bowing time and time again to the Asherah pole and to the statue of Baal. I read the stories and think, *Man! Can't they see what they're doing? They are sacrificing their life, the lives of their families, the future of their nation, and the destiny of their people because of an idol! I mean, it's a pole! Don't they see this?* Over and over again, generation after generation in history fall in this same way. King after king would repeat the sins of their ancestors and bow down in worship to these ridiculous idols. To me it is crazy! Who would do such a thing? That's when I hear the soft whisper of the Holy Spirit reminding me that I have idols in my own life to deal with—idols to which I too, was making significant and costly sacrifices. One of the biggest idols in my life has been my business and the ability to make wealth with it.

The fact is, being visually impaired has put me at a disadvantage in many types of situations and relationships. I can't just go out with a ball glove and toss around a baseball with my son, nor am I able to sit and watch a movie and point, laughing at the different scenes. Slapstick comedy doesn't work well for me. This is a difficult truth in my life presently. What I can do though, because of the business and the wealth it has brought, is give my family amazing experiences, such as Disney vacations and time on the beach. I can also provide for any material desire they or I may want. In my mind, it was a great way to level the playing field.

Then one day while I was on my knees in the presence of God, the Holy Spirit began to deal with me. He said, "Jeff, you have been deriving your identity from being a successful businessman, but now I am changing your focus. I am bringing you into the family business, and you will derive your identity from Christ." This was a powerful shift in my life, and I began to refocus on what was important. The truth is, the business is still going well; it's just not my primary focus any longer.

I believe the whole issue of identity is a crisis in our society today. We have generations of people who do not know who they are and are trying to seek this out in all the wrong places. Our world today provides many of these places. Confusion does not come from the Lord. But if the enemy can cause you to be confused about your identity, then he can prevent you from engaging in the fullness of your destiny. What's even worse is that whether or not you have children right now, your choices today will have an impact on all the generations that follow you.

Knowing who you are in Christ and passing this down to your children is critical. This makes it even more important to understand that whatever you idolize, you will become. That is why it is so important to identify the idols in our lives and then begin to replace them with right priorities.

First and foremost, is identifying who we are in Christ. It is only once our feet are firmly planted on this rock that we are able to weather the storms this life will bring. Trying to find your identity in anything else other than Christ is building your house upon the sand, and when the storm comes it will all collapse (Matthew 7:26–27). In a world where even the government is blurring the lines of identity, it is becoming increasingly difficult to develop a healthy one.

It is common knowledge that if you want to be healthy and strong physically, you must reflect this in your lifestyle. You cannot eat all the Doritos and tacos you want and still have that sought after six-pack. You need to make different decisions on a day-to-day basis of what you put into your body in order to change what your body will look like; as the saying goes, garbage in garbage out. This is the same with the spiritual person. We need to change and make good decisions on a day-to-day basis of what we choose to consume and worship. Just like a healthy lifestyle says you are what you eat, a healthy identity says you are what you worship. Keeping this point of view in mind, let's explore some of the common idols we find in our culture today.

One of the main idols currently, and you may have already guessed it, is the Internet. The Internet is a powerful force in the world today. It connects people from around the globe, and information can be sent in a millisecond from anywhere to anyone. It is a great tool for spreading the gospel! However, where there's a point, there's always a counterpoint, and with the Internet, this is more than the case. There are a lot of derogatory and dangerous things on the Internet that have become too readily available and too accessible by almost anyone. One such case in point is the area of pornography. Many men and some women struggle with this addiction.

With the proliferation of pornography on the Internet, making it easily accessible and completely anonymous, it has become a powerful idol because it is one that seemingly gives people full control over it. The falsehood of this, though, is the control is only for a very short time. Once the deed is completed, then the payment is extracted from their lives. I have seen many marriages break down and families destroyed because of men's choice to worship this idol.

The ramifications of pornography on our society are huge, much too large for this book to delve into. My advice to you if you are currently involved with it, is to turn from this idol immediately and ask God to deliver you from it. You may require time with a professional to go through a process of purging the images from your mind. You may also require an accountability partner or software on your computer to help you abstain. The men's organization Promise Keepers[8] is a great resource for these types of challenges, and I would advise you to get help right away.

The second major idol on the Internet is the prevalent group of social networks. The biggest of these is obviously Facebook. You can tell if you are idolizing Facebook if throughout the day you are constantly checking for updates and notifications or creating posts at a feverish pace. There is no set number to determine when you have crossed the line, but for me, it was a good indication that I had when my iPhone put my Facebook icon on my lock screen. It was time to do a Holy Spirit check in.

Have you ever had your child do something really cute or experience an event in your life, and rather than stopping and praising God and giving Him the glory for this, you think, *I should post this on Facebook!* This idol is one that can steal time from your family, almost imperceptibly to you, but glaringly to them.

The constant use of social media is becoming a real problem in our society today, so much so that there is even a term to describe it. In the news media, it is called *distracted parenting*. It is when a parent is physically with their children, but they are on their phone, predominantly on social media sites, rather than being present and engaged with their family. Approximately 3.2 hours a day of time on the Internet is spent on social media sites such as Facebook, Pinterest, and Twitter. This doesn't even include the time people are disconnected from life while they are connected to Reddit, YouTube, and Netflix, which can be categories of idolatry on their own.

The powerful truth about God, however, is that He can help us realign our priorities and cast down idols in our lives. I'm not saying Facebook is evil. On the contrary, it keeps me connected with friends and family around the world I would not regularly be in contact with, and that is a good thing. What I am saying is when it becomes a priority above your children, your spouse, and God, it has become an idol no better than an Asherah pole.

DEVELOPMENTAL KEY 8: Repentance

Another major idol on the Internet, especially for the younger generation, is online gaming like World of Warcraft, Black Hawk Down, Minecraft, and on and on it goes. People spend hours and hours at a time pouring their lives into a digitized world and communicating with people they have never and probably will never meet. I have seen this literally rip marriages apart. I have witnessed husbands and wives alike disappear into a room, not to be seen for a day or even two at a time, missing out on the outside world, and missing out on the family's life. If these are areas in which you admittedly struggle, you may have to get down on your knees and ask God for help in making the needed changes. Ask Him to help you unplug and reconnect with the people He has so graciously placed in your life. With His help, you can do things in your life you couldn't possibly do in your own strength. So much of our forward movement and momentum begins on our knees with the eighth developmental key of repentance.

In my job I have to be very connected to technology and be aware of what is coming in the future to make sure our business is properly positioned. One of the major developments that is coming is called Virtual Reality. I think this can be amazing, fun, and incredible! I also think this is a very real threat to our society and could cause individuals to slide further into isolation. The plan of the enemy of your destiny is to isolate you from the rest of the flock. Once you are isolated, it is easier to kill you.

Remember the scripture John 10:10? He comes only to do that very thing; to steal, kill, and destroy you. Jesus is very clear that this is a real danger, so much so that He's willing to leave the ninety-nine sheep to find the one. This is also shown in Luke 8 when Jesus went across the lake through a storm to find the demon-possessed man, the One who could provide him peace from his torturers—the Legion of demons.

If you add Virtual Reality to the aforementioned idols, it is a very potent temptation—one that could draw you into a single world where everything that exists is digital and fake. I emphasize I am not saying Virtual Reality is from the devil. On the contrary, it could be extremely fun and enjoyable. It comes back to how much time you are spending on these pursuits. I think the overriding issue is the time it keeps you away from God, from your family, your friends, from the outside world, and from serving the Kingdom. If you are spending more time alone than with other people, there is probably an idol in the midst.

Maybe you have balance in this area and you're saying, "That's not me! I spend lots of time with my family and my children." Then that is fabulous, but the one caution I would give you is that other common idols in our society are our family, spouse, or children. As important as these people are in our lives, if we revisit our priority list, we can acknowledge that if they take the position of God, they become an idol. I have known many parents who spent thousands of hours and thousands of dollars on their kids' sporting, musical, or artistic endeavors. These are not bad things in and of themselves, and I think it is important for children to be involved in these types of programs. But then the question becomes, *Are you over programming?* Is it taking the place of God in your life and in their lives? If you are running night after night, from place to place like a chicken with your head cut off, there is most likely a problem.

The final idol I would like to discuss, and perhaps the biggest one in our western culture by far is our self. Humanism has become so prevalent in our society that I would say it has become a driving force behind it. Society dictates that you can do what feels good, do what feels right, go ahead and have fun, no matter what the repercussions are, or whom your actions are impacting. In Isaiah 22:12–13, the scriptures warn the people that at a time when they should have been remorseful for their actions, they chose instead to follow the philosophy of "eat, drink, and be merry, for tomorrow we die." This is very much the same philosophy in which today's society is entrenched.

Humanism is self-worship. It says, *You are God*. And if you are God, then there's no one to whom you need to be accountable—no moral compass. You can blaze your own path and everyone else must be tolerant of it, for it is presumably your right and your choice. This option to do what you want without any morality or restrictions connects well with our sin nature. I believe this is the primary reason why humanism is so popular in our western culture. However, though it connects well with our sin nature, it does not connect well with God's plan for your life or your destiny.

The Walt Disney movie *Pinocchio* has an amazing storyline that depicts this current inclination. It characterizes a wooden boy who wanted to be something he was not. Pinocchio wanted to be a real boy, and he would do anything to change his self-image and who he was made to be—so much so that he found himself in the company of an evil fox who promised him all the fun and enjoyment a real boy would want.

The evil fox led him down the path to an amusement park. In this fun land, Pinocchio could do whatever his heart, or flesh, desired! He could play, eat, and even drink all the forbidden things in which parents would not allow their children to partake. Needless to say, he had a lot of company—the many other boys who also wanted to do what they wanted to do. I remember one scene in particular, where they were all playing pool and one boy was smoking a cigar and having a drink. All of a sudden, *Pop!* Out came the donkey ears and he began to heehaw like a pack mule. If you are familiar with the story, you know the boys ended up being the jackasses that had to go and work in the mine. Their frivolity was demanding its wages.

Throughout Pinocchio's whole ill-fated sojourn, his conscience, Jiminy Cricket, was warning him not to go. He tried to steer him away from this trouble. Obviously, Jiminy Cricket is a parallel to the Holy Spirit. Unfortunately, like Pinocchio, many people today do not listen to that still, small voice and they will eventually pay the price as he did.

This idol of humanism too, will extract its price at the right time. Just like I tell my children, there is no such thing as a free lunch, or in Pinocchio's case, a free ride, eat, and drink. You cannot serve two masters. At one point in time, both of them will require you to worship them exclusively. The mercy and awesomeness of Christ is that He gives the opportunity for you to make the choice. Deuteronomy 30:19 says, "Today … I have given you the choice between life and death … Oh, that you would choose life" (NLT).

With the onslaught of humanistic religion, we have also shifted from the fact that our physical bodies were made to worship, to worshiping our bodies themselves. People have therefore slipped into the trap that their bodies must be kept in a state as close to perfection as possible. This is why plastic surgery, diets, and gyms have become so extremely popular. We overindulge ourselves with food to make us feel good and then try to diet, workout, and even undergo surgery to rectify the natural consequences we reap. It's a crazy cycle.

In following this religion, we also have cast false images to idolize, not so different from the golden calf of our ancestors. Look at any fashion magazine for the unrealistically modified, airbrushed male or female models. This puts tremendous pressure on our younger generations, as well as the rest of society, to conform to such idealized, unrealistic images. This leads to such diseases as anorexia and bulimia. The darker side to this is reflected in the teenagers that slice up their flesh with a razor blade as they sit alone in their rooms, feeling rejected, believing they don't fit in and that they can't measure up to the falsely inflated standard of society. Some are so driven by the resulting feelings of worthlessness that they see no escape from the pain overtaking them; they see no way of making it better and thus fall victim to the lie of suicide.

The fact that the cosmetic industry is a multi-billion-dollar industry is proof of how much this idolatry has shaped our lives and has fashioned society in general. We don't want to be who we actually are, so instead we try to be someone, something else. I too, at one time fell prey to this amazing con of the enemy. I remember taking Creatine and other supplements to try to build bulk and muscle so I could look better for my potential wife. I would spend hours and hours in the gym trying to tone my body in all the right places to get the ever-elusive six-pack. I am happy to report I actually got that six-pack! It just has a layer of cushion over it to protect it. All kidding aside, this is a serious idol and one that can even seduce Christians.

We must be aware and alert to this insidious trap of the enemy. Remember, you are created in the image of God Himself, and God does not make junk. You are His masterpiece (Ephesians 2:10). Spend time with the Holy Spirit and ask Him to reveal to you who you are in Christ. Have Him show you the beauty and awesomeness of the creation you actually are. This is an important key in your development process on the journey to your destiny.

As this list of precautions is sizeable, you may begin to feel restricted, wondering if God is asking us to be a monk or a nun! No, this is not the case (unless, of course, that is your calling!) Always refer to the priority list of God first, spouse second, followed by family and work. Then fill in the excess time with the other things. It is fine to have many different things in your life to a measure (with the exception of pornography and humanism). The important thing is to achieve a godly balance—like the Bible says, we should live with moral excellence and self-control (2 Peter 1:5–6 NLT).

I realize this is a heavy topic, but take heart. We do not have to be overwhelmed by the lures and snares of idolatry set all around us by the enemy. We just have to be vulnerable and honest with ourselves and before the Father, laying it all out at His feet. Then we need to trust He will continually lead and guide us so we will become all He has planned for us to become. It is then we can live in the fullness of Christ and our destiny, with only the occasional leap of faith required!

CHAPTER 10

The Leap

I HAD ARRIVED. I TOOK A SECOND OR MORE TO ENJOY THE STUNning vista stretched out before me. While I was inhaling the sweet summer air of 1987, I could feel the breeze blowing through my hair, tussling it back and forth. It was a very hot day, and I could feel the warmth of the sun pounding down on me.

This feeling was short-lived and quickly overtaken by the greater sensation of the pounding of my heart in my ten-year-old chest. It became so loud to me it resembled those scary scenes in a movie when you knew something bad was about to happen, as the beating heart overtook the soundtrack: *thump, thump, thump, thump.* I felt like my heart was going to explode right out of my chest. I was standing on the top of a one-hundred-foot-high stony cliff, carved out of the great Canadian Rockies in the beautiful province of British Columbia.

If you were to follow the cliff wall down from where I was standing, it arched inward like a crescent moon, causing the top part to jut out about twenty feet farther than the bottom. In this arch, about twenty feet down from the top, there were dozens of birds nesting in the small, naturally formed orifices in the rock. From time to time there would be a great rustling noise and all of a sudden countless birds would come flying out in a huge flock from the arch of the cliff. This made my pending task of potential bravery far more terrifying, for at any moment, the birds could just swoop out from their rocky nests, and become an obstacle with which I could collide.

As your eye continued down the wall of the cliff, it would discover a pool of water. This pool was approximately half a mile wide, and about a one-hundred-stroke swim from the cliff edge to the shore, if you were a good swimmer. I was. The cool water was very deep. I would imagine it was at least as deep as the cliff was high. This made it about one hundred feet deep—deep enough to ensure a safe landing if one were to jump into it. This fact did not provide much relief to my pounding heart.

On the sand far below, there were many beachgoers lounging in their chairs. My family members were among them. This provided a significant audience, sitting on their towels, looking up at the cliff, and cheering on the jumpers. In the water itself were people on blow up rafts and inner tubes. They would chant, "Go, go, go!" for all those brave enough to take the giant leap. You see, people climb to the top of this towering cliff, and then jump off and land in the water far below.

Throughout that hot summer day, I had witnessed many people do this very thing. Some did it with a loud "Wahoo!" Others did it with a scream, but they still did it. To me, this looked exciting and fun. The only problem was, I was deathly afraid of heights, and I believed I could never jump off anything of a substantial height, let alone something with the extreme height of a one-hundred-foot cliff! This is a fear I had never shared with anyone.

As the afternoon wore on, my cousins kept talking about how awesome it would be to make the jump ourselves. I agreed, not wanting them to discover my underlying fear. However, I did find many convenient reasons not to go up the path to the top of the cliff. But, as the sun inched across the sky, I began to run out of excuses. My cousin was very persistent and finally convinced me to make the hike to the top. Actually, she pestered me to the top. I didn't want to be seen as weak or scared. That would be something I could never live down.

We had been discussing the prospect of making this huge leap all afternoon and wondered what it would be like. I showed myself pretty brave on the outside, but the inside did not follow suit. On the inside, I was as scared as a first-time skydiver taking that first horrendous step! As I walked up the path that led to the top of this big cliff, I was the vision of boldness, but the closer I got, the more anxious I grew. A knot was forming in the pit of my stomach that built with each step I took. When I arrived at the top and looked over the edge, the anxiousness turned into outright fear. It was like the fear was a large hand that wrapped itself around me, making it almost impossible to move.

So there I was, standing at the top of the cliff with the breeze flowing through my hair and my heart pounding out of my chest. I could hear the people below offering up their inspiration: "Come on, jump!" Over and over I ran right up to the edge—and then I would flat out stop. These several false starts encouraged more and more people to try to convince me to make this leap.

It was a tremendously scary prospect to make such a big leap without knowing what would happen when I hit the water. My mind generated assorted scenarios as the final outcome of the jump—all of them negative. In one of them, a large fish, bigger than any man on the beach, was just waiting for me to hit the water so he could sink his teeth into me and pull me down, never to be seen again. Another unnerving possibility was that I would go so far under the water I would not be able to make it back to the surface, and nobody would ever find me.

It's easy to laugh at it now, but at the moment it was very real and profoundly terrifying to me. Fear is usually irrational. I lost count of how many times I made these false starts. I would even speak to myself and say, "Come on, you can do this!" But it was like there was an invisible wall at the edge of the cliff preventing me from going over.

Mercifully, a man in an inner tube yelled up, "If you jump, I'll give you $100."

I yelled back, "$100 in real money? Cash, right now?" trying to get him to guarantee the strength of his offer. He agreed. Remember, I grew up extremely poor and back in the eighties that was a lot of money! So I backed up one more time about twenty feet from the cliff's edge, and I took a running start.

My feet pounded up and down on the packed earth. I was gaining momentum quickly, and before I knew it, I was at the edge of the cliff.

The momentum was enough that I no longer had a choice to just stop. I had to leap off the edge. I began to fall downward. The feeling was exhilarating and extremely scary all at the same time. I heard the wind whistling by my ears as the scene changed from clouds to treetops. It seemed like it took me hours to get from the top of that one-hundred-foot cliff to the water below.

All of a sudden, *splash!* My feet hit the water, and I went under. I remember thinking, *Wow, I'm going really deep! Does this thing have a bottom?* Then the downward momentum stopped, and the buoyancy of the water began to push me back up. I began to kick my feet and move my arms to get to the surface. I was so far down that I was struggling to get to the surface of the water before I ran out of oxygen. I also had to elude that massive fish, which was surely lurking just under me to bite my feet and pull me under. I began to swallow inside of my throat because the oxygen in my lungs was depleted, and I knew I had to get to the surface quickly. With a huge gasp, I broke the surface of the water and began to take in that sweet summer air again.

I cannot put into words the feelings of exhilaration, pride, and outright joy I experienced at that moment. Everybody around me was clapping and cheering. To say the least, it was an exciting and defining moment in my life. I went over to the man in the inner tube to collect my prize, and that's when he told me the bad news ... "Sorry kid, I was just kidding. I only said that to get you to leap off the cliff." I was mad! But the anger was incredibly short-lived. The truth is, as great as the money would have been to a ten-year-old boy, what that man gave me that day was much more valuable than money.

There was something else waiting for me at the surface of the water that day. It was victory over fear. I had learned how to take a leap of faith, and I discovered what it was like to reap the rewards after doing so. The exhilaration of being brave enough to face your fear, to take a leap of faith and to come out a conqueror is a life-changing experience. That day is forever engrained in my mind, and I'm very thankful to the man in the inner tube for unknowingly playing his role in my destiny.

I think my cliff jumping adventure makes a good analogy for many people who are at various points of the development process. Standing at the edge of the cliff, they are eyeing the pending leap, evaluating or even questioning the leap they may be required to take to initiate the next step in the process. But remember, submission to what the Father is asking is the key. Obedience will then release grace and forgiveness, which allows the Father's blessings to flow. Sometimes the submission to be obedient can be the most difficult part. But it is something He will call you to do over and over again throughout your life. And again, you should test the spirit and ensure you are indeed hearing from God before taking the jump.

The Bible says to count the cost before you build (Luke 14:28), but you also need to take the necessary steps forward as they are presented to you. God is the Master Developer and will move us from solution to solution along the path of our development process. I want to be clear on this point though: He will not force us. You have the free will to make the decision whether or not you will stay in or move on at any point while going through the process. This is actually why Jesus died on the cross—to make a way to the Father, set us free from our sin nature and provide us with a choice. The truth is we all still have two trees planted in the garden of our heart. Like Adam and Eve, we get to make the decision. The beauty of the grace of Jesus Christ is He allows us to redo it over and over and over again until we make the right one. His mercies are new every morning, and His grace is enough.

DEVELOPMENTAL KEY 9: Facing Your Fear

As you have read through this book and have reached this last chapter, you may now be thinking, *Yes, this was great for you and for other people in my life, but I could never do this.* If this is you, remember, sin will allow shame to enter in, and shame can become like a fog that will cloud your judgments and cause confusion. When this fog builds up enough, it rains down guilt and condemnation, pressing you to count yourself out of the good things God has for your life. This leads to rejection. Whether real or self-imposed, rejection or the fear of it, causes us to act out of fear, which will trigger the fight, flight, or freeze reactions, rather than responding in a godly manner. The enemy uses fear as a weapon to hold you back from engaging in your journey and from fulfilling your destiny.

The last thing the enemy wants is for you to walk fully in your destiny, because this crushes him under your feet and takes the kingdom away from him. He will whisper many things in your ear to stop you from making progress along the way. All along the path to the top of that cliff and the subsequent jump down, was a series of choices I had to make. If I had chosen not to go up the path or I had walked back down rather than making the leap, I would never have known what it felt like to face my fear and come out on top. I would never have known the exhilaration of what I'd been able to accomplish. In life we often have to do things despite our fear. Facing our fears, developmental key number nine, and doing things scared is how we grow. This is how we are stretched and how we are able to carry the mantle of our calling. The opposite of faith is fear and this is what the devil uses as a primary tool to stop you from moving forward. And this fear is often based solely on a lie.

I grew up watching the Tom and Jerry cartoon. If you can remember, Tom was a cat that was at least ten times larger than Jerry, the small brown mouse. In the show, they were archenemies, constantly at each other's throats. Most of the time Tom was the initiator, always trying to trap the poor little mouse. If Jerry found himself in a predicament in which he thought Tom was going to get his white-gloved paws on him and it would be the end of the road, he used the same old trick every time. He cast a shadow of a mean, scary dog on the wall. The false image of the dog was huge—much bigger than Tom. Jerry embellished the ruse of this fictitious shadow dog with mean growls and barks. The truth of the situation was it was just a tiny mouse casting a large shadow. The closer Tom got to Jerry, the smaller his mean shadow looked. Eventually, Jerry would have to flee.

This is the truth of paradigm and the effect it has on your perspective. The Bible is clear that the enemy prowls around like a roaring lion seeking whom he can devour (1 Peter 5:8). The truth is he is not a roaring lion; he just pretends he is. He does this to instill fear into you and hopefully distract you or stop you from your journey.

Things can seem much worse than they actually are until you face them. If you stop being in defense mode or being satisfied with just staying where you are, but rather begin to press into your calling, it will bring you closer and closer to whatever is casting the large shadow trying so desperately to deter you. The more you press into God and His calling, the smaller and smaller the enemy will look to you. Don't stop here! Keep pressing in!

While I was at the top of the cliff as a young boy, it seemed like it was one thousand miles to the water, but the truth was it probably took two seconds before I had hit the water and claimed the victory. This is the same truth available to you in your journey of development. The enemy is a liar and wants you to believe otherwise. If he can keep you in your fear, he can keep you from achieving your destiny. From where I stand now, it is hard to believe the impact fear almost had on my life and destiny. No one is immune. I only praise God He helped me to overcome.

Facing My Fear

In April 2007, the company for whom I had been working for before I had my own business was about to be sold. This was devastating news for me, as I had been offered a partnership in the business, and it was being sold before that promise was delivered upon. The company that was considering purchasing the business wanted to meet with the key individuals of the organization, me being one of them. During the initial calls and several subsequent meetings, they saw something in me, something I could not see in myself—a glimpse of my destiny, perhaps? They asked me if I would consider opening a dealership for them.

This was a huge and somewhat frightening proposition for me.

The company I worked for had been in business for almost a decade and had established a name and reputation in our city. The people who were looking to acquire the company had a different paradigm than I did. They were doing business on a national scale and had seen many different companies similar to ours. They knew what it took to make it work, and they could see my fear for what it really was—just a small mouse trying to stop me from taking the next step in my journey. However, I still couldn't see it. Sometimes it takes a loved one to point out our fears.

I was legally blind, and my wife and I had two small kids at home. We had a mortgage to pay, but no money to do so. I remember sitting in the hotel lobby of the Hilton Garden Inn with two individuals from this company, talking about opening this business. My mind was in overdrive. I was thinking, *Are you crazy? I can't do this.* I put up a myriad of different reasons why this couldn't make sense at this time. I saw it as being rational, not as fear.

On the other hand, my wife and co-laborer in destiny, who has always been a few steps ahead of me, knew the right thing to do. She knew I could do it and that we could be successful in the business. It makes me chuckle to think that if she was at the top of the cliff with that ten-year-old boy, she would have pushed him over the edge. That's what she did for me in this decision, and it was one of the best decisions we have ever made in our lives.

We have overcome insurmountable odds, and now, in our tenth year of business, we are one of the largest private security companies in the country. I acknowledge full well I could not have done this by myself. It is the Lord's help and the help of the people He put in my life, especially my wife, that made this possible. God knows exactly when to enlarge you. As a Master Developer, when the negative resembles the original picture, He will remove it from the solution and place it in an enlarger. Taking the small negative from the solution, God will stretch it into a bigger picture. The Father will take us through this enlargement process several times throughout the journey to our destiny. At this point, please note, though I advocate taking risks, it may have become apparent through reading this book that I am a person of balance, and the risks to be taken should be carefully measured and vetted by a multitude of counselors and the Word of God. However, if I had not made the leap and taken that risk, none of this would have happened. And I could not have taken the leap if my wife didn't show me that my fear was a small, insignificant lie that was magnifying itself within me. It was barking and snarling at me to try to prevent me from moving forward, but had absolutely no bite.

As a man thinks in his heart so he is, states Proverbs 23:7 (NKJV). The Bible also teaches that out of the abundance of the heart, the mouth shall speak (Matthew 12:34). To me, these verses speak to the notion that paradigm is everything when it comes to your development process. You need to allow yourself to be shown by the Holy Spirit how God, the original Photographer saw you at the inception of the original portrait. Once you have been given a glimpse or have received a portion of what that final photograph looks like, your paradigm shifts, and you gain a new perspective. You'll see fear for what it really is, and you will have the vision in your mind's eye to push toward. It is no different than running a race—a very long race.

Running the Race

My wife and I are marathon runners. Actually, she is a marathon runner, and I do it just to be with her. While I was writing this book, we were training for a half marathon that takes place in our city. We participate in this marathon every year, and she usually runs as my guide.

Being visually impaired makes it very challenging to run, especially outdoors. On a treadmill you know there's not going to be any sudden ground changes or people to crash into on the path. On this particular day, we had to accomplish twelve kilometers because we were nearing the 2/3 mark in our training plan. We had started the run along our regular route. At about 1.2 kilometers in, my wife noticed storm clouds were building in the distance and moving rapidly toward us. She is an avid weather observer. She has multiple weather apps, including one with radar, and she can tell you what is about to happen, when, and why. She was uncomfortable with what was happening so after running 1.5 kilometers we turned around and headed back toward our house. At this point, I had a decision to make. I knew there was a storm approaching, so I could go home and finish on the treadmill, or I could set my mind to finish my twelve-kilometer run outdoors on my own.

I decided to run with her back to our house but then decided to veer off the path to an area that had a loop on which I could complete my run. The loop was approximately half a kilometer long, so it would take a total of eighteen loops to make my total distance. I struck out to do this on my own. We see this in the story of Paul and Barnabas and their decision to split ways because of John Mark (Acts 15:39). This is not to say I am Paul and my wife is Barnabas, but the point is that along the path of your journey, people may come and people may go. You need to decide how that will affect you and whether or not it will alter your path to your destiny.

One, then two, then three laps went by. The storm had not yet started, but it was lurking close by. When you're running, you have a lot of time to think. My thoughts drifted to the time in the Bible when the storm rose up as Jesus and His disciples were crossing the lake (Matthew 8). As the storm began to rage, the waves tossed the boat about and began to break over the sides. The disciples panicked. They went to where Jesus was sleeping and woke him, shouting "Lord, save us! We're going to drown!" Jesus arose and looked at the situation. He rebuked the wind and the waves and calmed the storm.

The amazing thing about this is that at the beginning of the journey Jesus said they would cross to the other side. At that point, His disciples should have had the faith they'd make it to the other side, simply because Jesus spoke it. And now they were in the middle of the lake, with the water as still as glass. How are they going to get to the other side now? The wind and waves would no longer carry them. Simply put, they had to do it under their own strength; they had to row.

There is a strong lesson in this event. If we allow fear to control us in our decisions, we may have to do much more of our journey under our own strength. The better way, and I believe God's way, is to have faith in the Developer and be connected, through our destiny, to the supernatural power that God provides for us.

As God downloaded this revelation to me, there I was, about to run in a storm. I was on the fourth lap when the raindrops began to splat against the pavement. It started with random drops; one here and one there. And then the pace began to pick up—*splat, splat—splat.* Intermittent no longer, the rain began to steadily fall. I continued to push on ... lap six, seven, eight. Faster and faster the rain fell, and then I could hear thunder rumbling in the distance. The storm was going to be upon me; it was just a matter of time.

Lap ten. Lap eleven. Lap twelve. I continued to push on despite the storm that had now descended. Puddles emerged along my path. The rain, pouring now with a vengeance, made them invisible to my eyes. I would hear the splash as my runners became engulfed in water, thoroughly drenching my feet. If you run, you can relate: running in the rain with water-laden shoes is not a highly pleasant feeling. Lightning began to flash, and the sheets of rain echoed back.

At about lap fifteen, I had a decision to make. I could quit and go back home, or I could finish the final three laps. I evaluated the situation for safety, and I did not feel like I was in any imminent danger from the storm. I was nearing the end of my run, and it would have been easy to go home—the final few laps called understandably on account of rain. However, a switch flipped on in me at this point, and my determination had in an instant become stoic. I could imagine being on C4 on Everest. This is the final camp before the summit. The full force of the storm was still in the distance for the moment but was definitely going to encamp on the summit of the mountain. I believe there are two types of people in this world: those who talk about doing great things and those who actually take the risk, step out, and do them. I am definitely the second type.

Taking the risk doesn't mean you'll always succeed. I have had many failures in my life. But to have victory and achieve breakthrough, you must step out. You perhaps know the story of Thomas Edison. It took over three thousand designs to finally produce a practical, long-lasting electric light bulb that could be marketed commercially. He stepped out and persevered through the entire development process.

Having said this, I do recommend surveying whatever conditions you are in. Is there blue sky and sunshine, clouds and rain, or a tempest raging? It is imperative you're stepping out in the *right* conditions. The problem with this is many people can get stuck and never step out because the conditions will never be perfect. Note here, I said *right* conditions, not *perfect*. There is a significant difference between the right conditions and perfect conditions. The right conditions (though they are probably not perfect), create a window of opportunity. A window of opportunity is a certain time span you have to make a decision or choice whether or not to go forward with the opportunity as it is presented to you. Many people spend too much time gathering every minuscule detail and allow these opportunity windows to slam shut, never to be opened again.

In Matthew 14 (para), we read about the time when Peter is on the boat and sees someone walking on the water. He cries out, "Lord, if that's you bid me to come."

And Jesus said, "Come." Peter didn't pull out the spreadsheets, analyze them, evaluate and try to figure out all the logistics of the situation. There was no conversation such as, "Wow, look at those storm clouds. Those waves are pretty high. Are you sure we should do this?" No, he fully trusted Jesus, stepped out onto the water, and stepped into history as the only other man recorded in the Bible to actually walk on water. In the end, he did fall as he took his eyes off the Lord and focused on the circumstances around him, (which is an awesome lesson in itself), but he had stepped out of the boat.

So, if you were on Everest and you had an open window of opportunity, you would have a choice to make. You have one shot. One option is to turn back, leaving the years of training and preparation on the mountain, never to achieve the summit that has permeated your thoughts and dreams for so many years. Or, you could choose to face all your fears and take a calculated risk, which would require you to push on and reach the coveted summit.

If Jesus has said, "Come," and is calling you to take the risk, the choice, though still a choice, is strikingly clear, though perhaps not easy. This is why we cannot give up on our development process journey; we must finish.

With three more laps to go, I had made my decision: *I have come this far, and I was not going to quit.* I had decided to go for it; I had decided to finish what I had set out to do, regardless of the price I would have to pay. My quadriceps were aching, and with every forced step, I could feel the dull pain. Throbbing and splashing, the laps became more and more challenging. Still, I decided I would not be denied. At this point, I began to speak to myself. Sometimes in these types of situations, you have to get a bit crazy; you have to begin to speak to yourself. Paul encourages this in Ephesians 5:19 when he says to speak to one another in psalms, hymns, and songs. With no one beside me but the Holy Spirit, I began to motivate myself, saying, "I can do this! I will not be denied!"

Lap seventeen ... and then finally ... the crescendo ... the final lap was completed ... lap eighteen! Victory once again! It was exhilarating! It had been somewhat of a trial to complete that run. I had to run through the storm, through many, many puddles, and through the battlefield of my mind, but I finished what I had set out to do. Not much time would pass, and I would once again face the decision of taking a risk or walking away. And this time, so much more was at stake.

God of Miracles

As I stepped onto the red African dirt in Uganda, approximately four hours south of the equator, my mind was filled with disappointment. The Muslim governor of the district had called a last-minute holiday that wiped out the entire day of business meetings we had set up for our team from North America. Along with the crusades during the evenings, our team of Christian business leaders was to share practical business advice, faith stories, and Jesus with the leaders of the district. The last minute Muslim holiday scuttled all of this.

As a consolation, the owner of our hotel suggested we check out the hot springs located fifteen minutes away. He laughingly suggested maybe we could preach there. Our previous night's crusade translator was meeting with my pastor and decided to come with us. Oddly enough, as we walked to the van, he turned to me and said, "When you preach, I will translate for you." I laughed, replying that I was not preaching today. Besides, my pastor was the evangelist on this trip, not I.

Now, walking there on the red African soil, I looked around and out of my peripheral vision, I could see large rocks surrounding two pools of water. One pool was larger than the other. Navigating the large rocks, inclines, and declines was very difficult with my visual impairment. A couple of team members led me around to the small spring of water. The water came from an underground stream that was heated by a local volcano and was very hot to the touch. While this was happening, the Holy Spirit spoke to me about preaching the gospel in this place.

Imagine the scene with me. It was right out of a National Geographic film. The hot springs were surrounded by rocks all the way around and filled with African tribal people who came from every direction, some from many miles away. The local belief is that the waters have healing powers and if you were to bathe in them, you could be healed. These people were poor and very desperate. I knew the water had no healing power, but Jesus did. He was their only hope. I was stirred with compassion. Half-jokingly, I asked the interpreter if we could preach here. He hurried off and talked to whom I assumed was the chief of the area, and obtained permission for us to do so.

That was it. In an instant, I was committed. I had a choice either to do it scared or to look like a fool. You see, it had been my dream for many years to preach the gospel, and now I was in a moment where the opportunity was presented to me. I had a choice before me. What was I going to do?

My choice was made. I climbed up on a large rock, facing the people in the bigger pool. As I stepped onto the rock, the only way I can explain it is the Holy Spirit came upon me. I was not nervous. I actually felt empowered. My interpreter climbed onto a rock to my left, and one of my team members crouched down in front to prevent me from falling into the water.

I began to preach. I declared a simple but powerful message about Jesus and His healing powers. I told the story about the pool of Bethesda (John 5) where the first person to descend into the water after the angel stirred it, would be healed. Then I explained that Jesus died for our sins, and if they invited Him from the outside to the inside, He could forgive all their sins and heal all their diseases—every one of them. I preached for only about five minutes and then gave a salvation call. One hundred percent of an estimated one hundred and fifty to two hundred souls gave their lives to Jesus! I did not stop there. I was compelled to pray for healing. Since my message assured them He could heal all of their diseases, I began to pray for them. At first I was calling them out of the water, not realizing many of them were naked! One of my team members quickly suggested a general prayer. I did this, and many people said they were healed right then and there.

After the general prayer, countless people left the water, dressed, and came up to us for more specific healing needs. The miracles began. Many diseases were healed. I personally witnessed two blind ladies receive their sight, just like that. This had an incredible impact on me due to my own visual impairment. I don't profess to understand how healing works; I just know God still heals today. We saw a woman limp up to us, dragging her crippled leg behind her. This leg lacked most of its muscle mass. Right under our praying hands, we could feel the muscles grow back, and she walked away under the power of both legs. Dozens of other miracles were performed as our entire team prayed over the people. It was like a scene from the Book of Acts. One of our team members gave a Bible to a man who said he was going to plant a church on that very spot. If I was not there and it was not all caught on video, I would have had a hard time believing it myself. But God is an amazing God, and He longs to do amazing things with all of us.

As we left, a man pursued us, yelling and demanding money. Our interpreter said this was the local witch doctor, and we had just put him out of business. As we drove back to our hotel, my mind was racing, and all I could say was, "Wow!" I had connected with something huge. I had connected with my destiny. It didn't look like I thought it would, but this is what I was destined to be and to do. I had taken what for me was a big risk and did it afraid, but God poured out on us in an amazing way. It was not the pinnacle, but it was a destination point well on the way to my destiny! And this is how God designed it to be; leading, guiding, and connecting us to the power we are availed as we walk in our destiny.

In the End

This is the way I see the journey of the development process. Many people need to just begin the journey; take that initial step. You may be standing at the top of your very own cliff, paralyzed by that same hand of fear that had me gripped at the top of my own cliff. I encourage you to just go forward and boldly make the leap, trusting God, even if you are afraid. Or maybe you had made the leap and have hit the water, and now you're struggling for air as you fight to get back to the surface. This may be just for a season, but you need to battle and contend for your breakthrough. Or perhaps you have had a breakthrough, and the reward you expected to receive was different than what you actually received. Maybe you need to walk through forgiveness and the release of expectation in order to finish your race strong.

If we think of Paul, at the end of his life, he was in chains in Rome for the Gospel (Colossians 4:3). The Lord told him to go to Rome, and he obeyed. His obedience rendered him locked in chains. In the natural, this makes no sense. We do not understand how this could be a fitting reward for someone who unwaveringly stood for God. This, however, was the most fruitful season in Paul's life. Much of the New Testament was written while he was in jail. It is amazing to read Paul's wise counsel to Timothy at the end of his life. He didn't talk about bitterness and disbelief because of where he ended up. On the contrary, he encouraged Timothy to run his race well and to finish strong (2 Timothy 4). This exhortation was given to a young man at the beginning of his journey by an old man, in chains for the Gospel, nearing the end of his.

So you may be young and at the beginning of your journey, you may be at C4 about to make your summit run, or you may be on the eighteenth lap nearing the end of your race. There may be storm clouds forming in the distance. The rain may already be falling around you. The gates of hell may be trying to stop you. You may be like Joseph and find yourself in a pit. Or maybe you have had something significant snatched from you in an unjust situation like Joseph in Potiphar's house. Maybe you find yourself in a jail cell, placed there in your innocence. You may have to get crazy and start speaking to yourself.

No matter the circumstance, you need to run hard and push through to the finish! I encourage you to be one of the finishers so, like Paul, you too can say, "I finished the race" (2 Timothy 4:7 NLT). Be one of those who finishes this race strong, pushing through hard until the very end. Do it! Yield to the Master Developer. Engage with the keys to unlock your potential, and walk through the destination points. Complete the journey in the process of development for the expansion and victory of the Kingdom of God! Your next breakthrough is closer than you think. He will take you from the pit to the palace. Trust Him. He is causing all things to work together for good in your life.

Commissioning Prayer

We have made it to the end. You have read the book and hopefully have chosen to make the leap and begin your development process, or continue to step out in it. In these pages I have poured out my heart and life with the hope it would inspire and help you to be more than you are—inspire you to fulfill your destiny. Remember, this is the beginning, and you have an amazing journey in front of you, no matter where you come from or where you are right now. So get excited! He has big things planned for you! In conclusion, I would like to pray over you and release you into the fulfillment of your calling in Jesus Christ.

Father, in the name of Jesus I come before You, and I ask You to release Your Holy Spirit over the person reading these words right now. You are a God who knows no time or distance, and wherever they may be in the world or in their life's journey, I pray You will cause all things to work together for good for Your glory.

I pray as they walk through the development process and wounds are uncovered, that Your Holy Spirit would touch and heal them, causing them to be able to move forward stronger than before. I pray You would bring the mountains in their life down and raise up the valleys. I ask You to cause their paths to be straight and level. I thank You that no weapon formed against them shall prosper and that You have made them the head and not the tail.

I thank You that You are causing them to go over and not under. I pray You would release angels to be about them, to guard and protect them, and to move them forward in the process of development. I rebuke the enemy from their lives and the devourer from their finances. I release abundance, increase, and blessing in the mighty name of Jesus. Father, I pray You would surround them with people who are to be a part of their destiny—members of their team. Send the right people into their lives at the right time. I thank You that the person reading this book right now is a world changer, a nation shaper, and the very gates of hell cannot stand against them. I pray for victory and power in their lives. I pray this all in the mighty name of Jesus Christ our Lord! Amen!

All the best, Jeff Barnhardt
All praise and glory to God!

If this book has blessed you, would you help me out by leaving a review by clicking the link below. Even a one sentence review will help the book get into the hands of other readers and bless them too. Thank you in advance!

www.amazon.com/Destined-Be-Purpose-Unlocking-Potential-ebook/product-reviews/B01MU6340G

APPENDIX

Developmental Keys

THE DEVELOPMENTAL KEYS ARE NOT LISTED IN THE ORDER OF importance, but reflect the chronological order in which they are discussed. These keys never function in isolation, but are interconnected and operate in conjunction with each other. Often one will not come without the other. They will need to be used over and over again as new situations arise in your life, and as healing and growth occur.

DEVELOPMENTAL KEY 1: Submission and Obedience

DEVELOPMENTAL KEY 2: Perseverance

DEVELOPMENTAL KEY 3: Unity

DEVELOPMENTAL KEY 4: Faith

DEVELOPMENTAL KEY 5: Trust

DEVELOPMENTAL KEY 6: Forgiveness

DEVELOPMENTAL KEY 7: Identity

DEVELOPMENTAL KEY 8: Repentance

DEVELOPMENTAL KEY 9: Facing Your Fear

Notes and Resources

1. English Oxford Living Dictionaries. *en.oxforddictionaries.com*.

2. Merriam-Webster online Dictionary. *www.merriam-webster.com*.

3. Collins, Jim. *Good to Great: Why Some Companies Make the Leap*. New York: Harper Business, 2001.

4. Meyer, Joyce. *Battlefield of the Mind*. Nashville: Faith Words, 2005.

5. Well, Joel. Sermon. *www.harvestcity.ca*. July 17, 2016.

6. Harrison, Diane. *The Power of Prophetic Teams*. Belleville: Guardian Books, 2013. (Accompanying workbook).

7. The Genesis Process. *www.genesisprocess.org*.

8. Promise Keepers. *www.promisekeepers.ca*. *www.promisekeepers.org*.

Jeff Barnhardt is a husband to Andrea and a father of four children. He is a best selling author, speaker, and award-winning entrepreneur. He has ministered to the body of Christ and business leaders in many countries around the world. Jeff currently serves as president and CEO of a privately held security company he founded with his wife.

His passion is to help people discover their life's purpose while empowering them to unlock their God-given potential.

Connect with Jeff at:
Website: *www.jeffbarnhardt.com*
Facebook: *www.facebook.com/JeffRBarnhardt*
Twitter: *@jeff_barnhardt*

Made in the USA
Monee, IL
05 February 2021

59709324R00085